Stone Age Nottinghamshire

David Budge and Chris Robinson

Series editor - *Virginia Baddeley*

Nottinghamshire
County Council

David Budge has long been interested in old things, as a small child being fascinated by dinosaurs and ruined castles. He got his first taste of excavation with the Derbyshire Archaeological Society and soon became obsessed with lithics. After spending time studying at Nottingham University he worked for a variety of contracting archaeological units and is currently part of the Conservation Team at Nottinghamshire County Council.

Chris Robinson studied archaeology as a mature student at the University of Nottingham graduating in 2003 with a PhD in Archaeological Materials, specialising in early high temperature industries, especially glass and faience. Currently, Chris is a professional archaeologist who works as a member of the Nottinghamshire County Council Conservation Team.

© Copyright: Nottinghamshire County Council 2011

All rights reserved. No part of this publication may be reproduced, stored or introduced into a retrieval system or transmitted in any form or by any means (electronic, mechanical, photocopy, recording or otherwise) without permission from the publishers.

Whilst every care has been taken to ensure the accuracy of the information contained in this publication, Nottinghamshire County Council cannot accept any responsibility for any error or omission.

ISBN: 978 0 902751 70 5

Printed and designed by: Design, Publications and Print, Nottinghamshire County Council

Front cover: Clockwise from top: engraving of stag, Creswell Crags; tanged point from Creswell Crags; antler harpoon point from the Trent; bone pin from Creswell Crags; Creswell point from Creswell Crags; view of Creswell Crags; Neolithic antler maceheads and polished stone axe; handaxe from Beeston. *DJB*
Title page: Early Upper Palaeolithic blade points from Creswell Crags *DJB*
Back cover: Mammoth steppe, with typical animals of this habitat.
Mauricio Anton/Creative Commons

Contents

Acknowledgements

Thanks are due to the following individuals who have provided help and assistance:

Dominic Andrews, Rachel Atherton, Helen Berry, Andrew Curtis, Rebecca Dunn, Mary Fraser, Daryl Garton, Graeme Guilbert, Ann Insker, Roger Jacobi, David Knight, Neil McNabb, Graham Mullan, Peter Robinson, Ken Smith, Maria Smith, Ursilla Spence, Greg Speed, Ian Sutton.

Dedication
Chris would like to dedicate his chapter to Andy Haynes and Shaz Robinson for completely different yet equally vital reasons. David would like to dedicate his chapters to The Parents, not least for putting up with all the flint.

Originators of images are indicated beside each one. Abbreviations are as follows:

CHT - courtesy of Creswell Heritage Trust

CUCAP - original photograph held at Cambridge University Collection of Aerial Photography

DJB - David James Budge, Nottinghamshire County Council

DMG - courtesy of Derby Museums and Art Gallery

DOM - courtesy of Doncaster Museum and Art Gallery

EG – Emily Gillott, Nottinghamshire County Council

KDB - Kenneth David Budge

NAA - courtesy of Northern Archaeological Associates

NC - Nick Crouch, Nottinghamshire County Council

NCMG - courtesy of Nottingham City Museums & Galleries

TPA - reproduced by permission of Trent and Peak Archaeology

UBSS - courtesy of University of Bristol Spelaeological Society

UM - courtesy of The Manchester Museum, The University of Manchester

Creative Commons:

Woolly Mammoths - © 2008 Public Library of Science.
Sedwick C (2008) What Killed the Woolly Mammoth? Image copyright: Mauricio Anton.
Howick – http://www.geograph.org.uk/photo/1091110 . Image copyright: Andrew Curtis.
This work is licensed under the Creative Commons Attribution-Share Alike 2.0 Generic License. To view a copy of this license, visit http://creativecommons.org/licenses/by-sa/2.0/ or send a letter to Creative Commons, 171 Second Street, Suite 300, San Francisco, California, 94105, USA.

Time charts are based upon:

North Greenland Ice Core Project members, 2004, 'High-resolution record of Northern Hemisphere climate extending into the last interglacial period', *Nature*, vol 431, No 7005, pp 147-151.

Shackleton, N.J., Berger, A. and Peltier, W.R., 1990, 'An alternative astronomical calibration of the lower Pleistocene timescale based on ODP Site 677', *Trans. R. Soc. Edinburgh, Earth Sci.,81: 251-261.*

Shackleton, N.J. and Pisias, N.G., 1985, 'Atmospheric carbon dioxide, orbital forcing, and climate' in: E.T Sundquist and W.S. Broeker (eds), *The Carbon cycle and atmospheric CO2: natural variations Archean to present*, Geophysical Monograph 32, 412-417.

Map of Doggerland is based upon:

Coles B, 1998, 'Doggerland: a Speculative Survey', *Proceedings of the Prehistoric Society*, vol 64, pp 45-81.

Gaffney, V, Fitch, S and Smith, D. 2009, *Europe's Lost World. The Rediscovery of Doggerland*. CBA Research Report 160.

Please note: Two pence coins included in the photographs of objects are there to help illustrate the size of those objects.

Introduction

The first book in our series of guides to the archaeology of Nottinghamshire covers the time often known as the Stone Age, because metals had not yet been discovered and tools made of stone were widely used instead. This distinction was made when antiquarians first began to study the distant past. As knowledge progressed, it became clear that this stage had lasted for many thousands of years, during which huge changes had taken place. Consequently, the Stone Age was subdivided into three periods: the Palaeolithic (meaning old stone age), Mesolithic (middle stone age) and Neolithic (new stone age). Further study has revealed even more distinctions and so for example the Palaeolithic period has been divided into three: the Lower Palaeolithic (earliest), Middle Palaeolithic and Upper Palaeolithic (most recent). Of course the divisions that we have invented would have meant nothing to the people living at the time. They didn't wake up one morning to find that farming had arrived and it was now the Neolithic period, instead change often came gradually over many years. As our knowledge moves on we may well have to change our description of the distant past again; indeed the division between the Neolithic period and the following Bronze Age (to be covered in the next book) is looking increasingly blurred, with more continuity than change.

The period covered by this book is vast, from the time of the earliest inhabitants of the area that is now Britain at possibly 1 million years ago to the transition into the Bronze Age, at around 2,050 BC. That leaves only a further 4,050 years to get us to the present day (see the timeline inside the front cover).

Just as the time scale is vast, so too are the climatic changes that have taken place. The Palaeolithic period covered by the first part of this book falls into the era known as the Pleistocene, the time of the ice ages. The Earth's climate naturally oscillates between cold phases (glacials) and warm phases (interglacials), due to a 'wobble' in its orbit. Many glacials and interglacials occurred in this era of earth's history, but we are only concerned with the very last ones, in which early and modern humans were present in the area which was later to become Britain. After this stage we come into the modern era, called the Holocene, during which the climate has remained generally similar to what we see today. However, it is possible that we are just living in another interglacial, with more cold phases still to come.

In writing this guide, we have tried wherever possible to use examples from Nottinghamshire. Sometimes this just isn't possible, especially for such distant times when often there's very little evidence to go on, and then we have referred to sites from all over Britain or even further afield, if they will help to explain what life was like. We have also included some background chapters, about stone technology, the River Trent and Doggerland to help set the scene.

Lithic Technology

No book on prehistory would be complete without consideration of stone tools and lithic technology. The term lithic means 'of stone' and it is used to describe tools made out of stone, and the techniques used to make them.

Stone was the most durable material used by our prehistoric ancestors. The oldest surviving man-made objects are chipped stone axes from Ethiopia, well over two million years old. Our ancestors exploited a wide variety of raw materials to create their tools and equipment, but normally the bone, leather, sinew, wood, fur, plant material and antler they used have decayed away, leaving nothing but the pieces of chipped stone.

Even though so much has been lost, studying their stone tools can still reveal a great deal of information about people in the past. As the technologies to make them changed over time, and are associated with different groups (and even different species), it is possible to use these objects to date archaeological sites and to say something about the people who made them. Studies of the raw materials they used can tell us the sort of territories those groups ranged through or even provide hints of trade or gift exchange networks. Microscopic analysis of damage to tool edges can reveal what sort of material was being worked by the tool and how that was being done. In the earliest periods, before the arrival of modern humans, study of the way tools were made can tell us something about how our earliest ancestors could think and act.

Certain types of rock fracture in a very predictable manner when struck and so can be worked into tools. The way that the stone fractures has a characteristic form and is said to be conchoidal (literally 'shell-like'). The rocks most commonly used in Britain were flint, chert and quartzite, all of which were worked by flaking. Flint and chert are quite easy to work and can produce very sharp edges. Quartzite is harder to work than flint and chert and tends to produce cruder flakes which become blunt more rapidly. It is not really suitable for finely worked artefacts like arrowheads but is good for core tools such as handaxes. In areas where flint is scarce (e.g. Nottinghamshire) large cobbles of quartzite were easy to find and could produce much larger flakes than the smaller flint nodules which were available. As well as their use for making tools, quartzite pebbles were also widely used as hammer stones throughout prehistory.

In the Neolithic period, some types of stone which could not be worked by flaking were used to make polished axes. These were shaped by 'pecking' them into the desired form, which would then be finished off by grinding and polishing.

For a quick guide to the major types of each period, see colour plate, page 34.

Methods

Knapping - The process of making a flint or stone tool by striking or applying pressure to remove flakes from a larger block, then using either the flakes or the piece they were removed from. The person doing this is called a knapper.

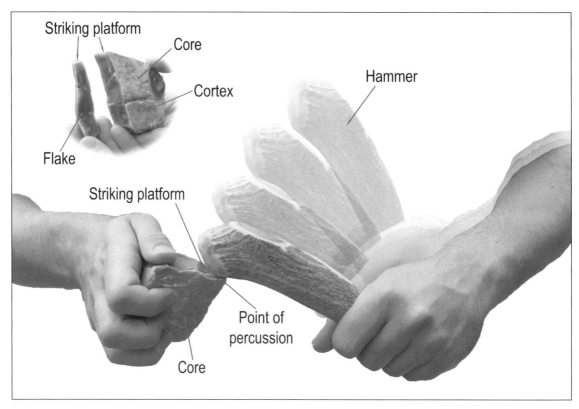

Knapping
DJB/KDB

Hard hammers - Hammers which are of similar hardness to the stone being flaked. The most commonly used stones for hard hammers in prehistory were quartzite and flint. They can be recognised by the areas of crushing which are usually present on one or more ends. Flakes produced by using a hard hammer usually have wide platforms and a pronounced bulb of percussion, with noticeable shock rings radiating out from this.

Soft hammers - As the name suggests, these are made of materials which are much softer (relatively) than the stone being struck. The most commonly used material was antler, and a piece of a 500,000 year old antler soft hammer has been found at Boxgrove, West Sussex. In addition to antler, hard woods, bone and soft stones (like sandstone) could be used. Soft hammers can be identified by the wear and small chips of flint embedded in the business end. Flakes produced using a soft hammer generally have a narrow platform, and small, diffuse, bulb of percussion. Soft hammers are used for finer work than hard hammers and were used for jobs such as making fine hand axes, blades and daggers.

Pressure flaker (retoucher) - In addition to direct percussion (bashing the stone with a hammer), stone can also be worked by applying pressure to detach flakes. Pressure flakers were usually made of antler or splinters of antler. The Iceman, a late Neolithic man discovered frozen in a glacier on the Austrian / Italian border, had a pressure flaker in his tool kit. This basically looked like a large pencil, being a circular piece of wood with a splinter of antler inserted in the end. As the end of the antler wore away through use, the flaker could be sharpened like a pencil to reveal fresh antler. Flakes detached by pressure flaking still have all the characteristics of a struck flake (bulbs and rings) but are usually rather small, as it is difficult to detach flakes any longer than a few centimetres. Pressure flaking was used for fine work, such as making arrowheads or retouching knives.

Tools for knapping – hard hammers, soft hammer, abrader and pressure flaker.
DJB

A fine pressure-flaked Neolithic arrowhead, from Holme Pierrepont.
DJB/Graeme Guilbert

Abrading stone - A piece of sandstone or other abrasive stone, used to rub platform edges to strengthen them. If a platform has thin, sharp edges or points it may shatter when struck, so in periods where people were taking care over their knapping they used abraders to remove such sharp edges to prevent failed removals.

Retouch - Deliberate modification of the edge of a struck flake, either by direct percussion or by pressure flaking. Depending on the angle at which it is applied, retouch can be used to sharpen flakes, blunt them or even shape them.

Terminology

Axe and adze - Core tools used for chopping. An axe has the blade mounted in the same axis as the handle, while an adze has the blade at 90 degrees to the handle. Both were used in the same way as their modern counterparts, probably mostly for woodworking.

Blade - A flake which has a length which is more than twice its width. True blades should have parallel sides and will usually have one or more ridges which are also parallel with the sides.

Burin - These tools have had one or more flakes removed to leave a strong, chisel-like edge. They were used for working antler and bone.

Burin showing burin spalls removed to make the strong, sharp edge
DJB

A burin in use.
DJB

Core - The piece of stone from which flakes have been removed. Cores have many negative scars from the flakes which have already been removed but should not themselves have a bulb of percussion.

Core tool - A tool made by removing flakes from a nodule. Axes and adzes are examples of core tools.

Cortex - The outer skin of a flint nodule. This ranges from thick and chalky when the flint is near the source, to a very thin smooth layer when the flint has been transported some distance from the source by glaciers and water. The surface of struck flint gradually changes colour and texture over a very long time, appearing to change back into cortex. The rate of change depends on the soil type but, as a rule, the more corticated a piece is, the older it is.

Flake - A piece of stone struck from a core. This may have the scars of previously removed flakes on the dorsal surface (back) or may have the outer surface of the nodule (the cortex), but will always show a bulb of percussion or shock rings on the ventral surface.

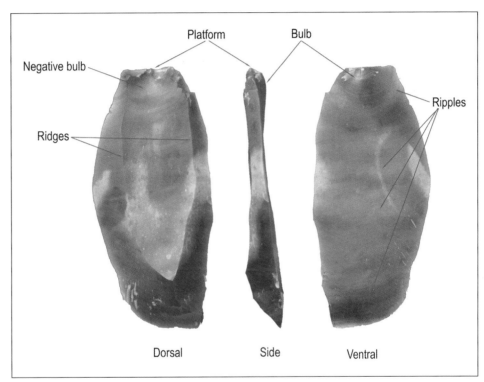

Anatomy of a flake. *DJB*

Flake tool - A flake which has been retouched into a tool. Scrapers, knives and piercers are all examples of flake tools.

Handaxe - A type of core tool, the 'Swiss army knife' of prehistory. Handaxes could have a variety of uses including digging and woodworking, but were mainly used for cutting and butchery. They were held in the hand and were not hafted.

Knife - A retouched tool designed for cutting. Knives have a cutting edge with an angle of less than 45 degrees. The cutting edge may be retouched to make it stronger or may be left unmodified (sharper but weaker) with the opposite edge blunted to aid in handling / hafting.

Microlith - A small tool made by retouching a blade. They occur in a variety of shapes, from being simply truncated across one end to create a sharp point, to a variety of very small geometric forms. Microliths were hafted and were used for a variety of purposes, from cutting tools and drills to projectile tips.

Piercer / borer and awl - These are two separate types of tool but both have pointed ends and were used for making holes in a variety of substances, such as wood, bone or hide. Awls were made by retouching one side of the point, then turning the piece over and retouching the other side, while piercers have both sides of the point retouched from the same side. Awls were used to cut a hole by being rotated in one direction, a bit like a modern drill, while piercers were rotated back and forth in both directions.

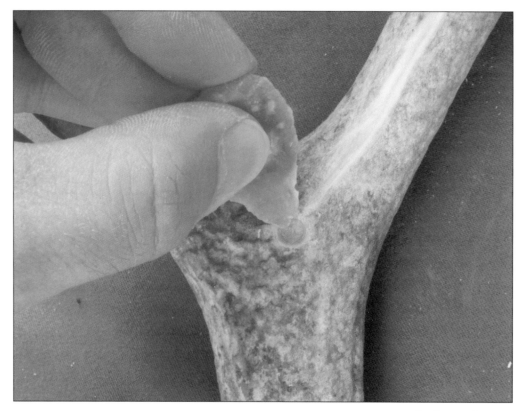

A piercer in use.
DJB

Scraper - The commonest tool type found on prehistoric sites. Made from a flake where steep retouch has been applied to give a strong, sturdy edge which has an angle of more than 45 degrees. Scrapers were mostly used for hide processing, scraping off all the fat and tissue to prepare the skin for use in clothing or for making equipment. They may also have been used in woodworking. Some scrapers may have been hafted, while others were held in the hand.

Waste flake - A flake which was produced during knapping but which was not the desired product and was not used. For example, when making an axe, the flakes removed are waste flakes as the axe is the end product.

The River Trent

Arguably, Nottinghamshire's greatest asset is the Trent. In the past, before the building of the reliable road and railway networks we now take for granted, rivers were the main highways across the land. Throughout most of prehistory after the ice age, landscape obstacles such as thick forests and marshland made travel difficult and the rivers provided the most convenient routes. From the Neolithic period onwards, there are finds of boats in the form of dugout canoes, made out of large logs. There are no boats from earlier than this, but there is plenty of indirect evidence, including Mesolithic burials located on what are known to have been islands at the time and bones of deep-water fish found in late Mesolithic shell middens of the North of Britain and Denmark. People who were able to go out to sea to fish would presumably be able to negotiate a river.

In addition, the range of resources offered by rivers made them attractive locations for habitation, and in later periods, after the adoption of farming, flooding provided rich and fertile soils for cultivation.

The Trent that we see today is constrained by locks, weirs and floodbanks and it no longer wanders as it used to. In the distant past its course was quite different, and before around 400,000 years ago it did not exist.

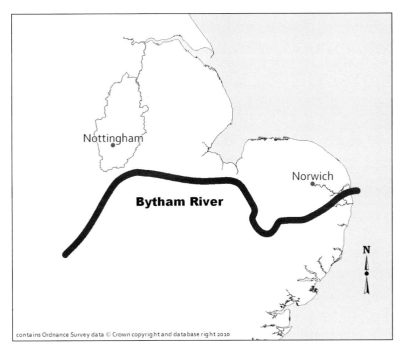

contains Ordnance Survey data © Crown copyright and database right 2010

Part of the course of the Bytham river, based on sections exposed during gravel quarrying.
After Gaffney et al, 2009, fig 1.17

The evolution of the Trent began as a result of changes to the landscape caused by ice. The most extreme glaciation in the last 700,000 years was the Anglian, around 450,000 years ago. At the height of the Anglian glaciation all of Britain north of the present Thames was covered by ice; in the area which is now Nottinghamshire it was over a mile thick. This glaciation was of major importance in shaping the modern landscape. Prior to this, the area was drained by a massive lost river known as the Bytham which flowed from west to east. This river ran to the south of where Nottinghamshire now is, through Norfolk and into Doggerland.

The power of ice is impressive. The Anglian ice sheets obliterated the Bytham river and swept the landscape of Nottinghamshire clean. As the glaciers retreated, a new pattern of drainage developed on the landscape which emerged from under the ice. This was the birth of the Trent, although in this period it flowed east from Newark to pass through the Lincoln Gap, rather than north to join the Humber as it does today. The earliest of the gravel deposits, or terraces, along the Trent come from this period. Though there have been a number of glaciations since then, which altered the course of the Trent to varying degrees, they were never powerful enough to completely obliterate the Trent and produce a fresh start as the Anglian glaciation did with the Bytham.

The Trent looked rather different in the distant past than it does today. During the cold phases meltwater from glaciers and the lack of vegetation meant that the river ran in multiple braided channels, moving over a wide area and changing course frequently due to floods and blockage by ice or debris. During warm phases, and after the end of the ice age, the more regular flow of water led to the river cutting more deeply into its floodplain, producing a landscape with one or more active channels winding their way across the whole of the floodplain, among a network of abandoned channels and cut off meanders in various stages of silting up. Forests grew up along the banks and big floods could uproot large trees, which are sometimes found preserved in gravel quarries. The Trent has a large catchment area which includes extensive areas of high ground in Staffordshire, Derbyshire and Leicestershire so it has always been prone to flood when meltwater or heavy rain comes rushing in.

A large braided river outwash plain,
Alaska. The Trent could have looked
very like this at the end of the Ice Age.
I Sutton

The Trent was a major factor in the prehistoric settlement of the region and has also affected the nature of the evidence that is left behind. For the earlier periods of prehistory, a large proportion of evidence we have in Nottinghamshire has come in the form of stone tools found among gravels laid down by the river.

The river also provides us with precious evidence for past environments, in the deposits left behind when an abandoned river channel silts up. These features are known as palaeochannels. The silts trap pollen which is blown in from the surrounding area, as well as beetles and other insects living in the water or washed in from nearby. Waterlogged conditions preserve wood and other organic material which may include animal or even human bone, as at Staythorpe (Mesolithic) or Langford (Neolithic). All this information reveals a picture of the local and sometimes the wider landscape that would otherwise be impossible to find.

Doggerland - Europe's Atlantis

Within the first couple of thousand years following the end of the last cold phase, starting around 10,000 years ago, Europe lost what amounts to an entire country, larger in area than modern Britain. This land now lies beneath the North Sea and has been named 'Doggerland' by archaeologists, after the Dogger Bank where many bones and artefacts have been trawled from the seabed in the nets of fishing vessels over the years. Doggerland linked modern Britain to the Continent and at its greatest extent, during the early Upper Palaeolithic, its coast line was located as far north as what are now the Shetland Isles, which were then just a range of hills.

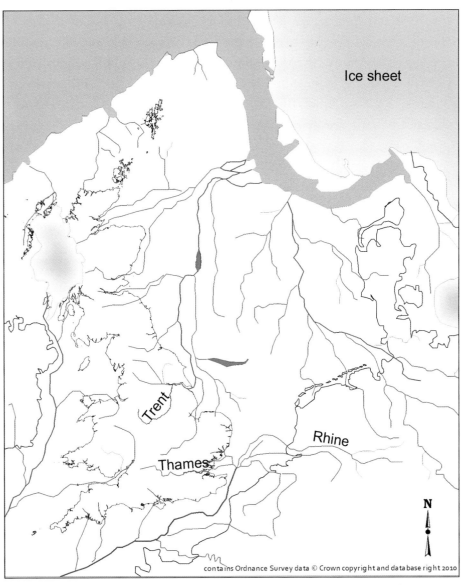

Doggerland at its greatest extent, during the Devensian Cold Phase.
After Coles 1998 and Gaffney et al 2009

The reason Britain and continental Europe exist today is because they were the high ground, the hills and mountain ranges, while Doggerland was the low land, the plains, river estuaries, lakes and coastlines which were inundated as the seas rose. For people living a hunting and gathering lifestyle, these were perfect places to live. The plains supported herds of game; lakes provided a rich source of fish, wildfowl and useful plants and they attracted animals which came to drink and could be ambushed. The estuaries especially provided such a richness of resources that they were the first places in the landscape to have seen long term, permanent or semi-permanent settlement. There, people had access to both terrestrial and marine resources such as fish, shellfish, sea birds and marine mammals (such as seals). In contrast, the highlands, mountain ranges and hills of what is now Britain were ventured into in pursuit of migrating animals and other resources, but would never have provided the same level of resources as the lowlands.

Doggerland was lost at the end of the last ice age, when the warming climate resulted in the melting of glaciers and the retreat of the polar ice caps. This led to massive sea level rise of around 120 metres over just a few thousand years. The seas began to rise in the Upper Palaeolithic period, around 18,000 BC, but the most dramatic period of rise (and consequently land loss) took place in the Mesolithic period, starting about 8,000 BC. The last of parts of Doggerland finally disappeared beneath the waves as sea levels approached current levels at around 5,500 BC. Britain became a group of islands and has remained so ever since, with communication with the Continent only possible by boat.

Obviously these changes would have had a drastic effect on the residents of Doggerland. At times, sea level rise would have been so rapid that people would have seen rich ancestral hunting grounds disappear beneath the rising waters during their lifetimes. When water broke through natural features (such as hills protecting low lying ground or valleys), inundation could have been so rapid as to sweep away any settlements that were present. It can only be guessed what sort of impact this would have had on the people's spiritual and religious outlook, as well as their way of life. The loss of the rich lowland resources as the seas advanced would certainly have driven people into the more marginal lands, causing pressure on the resources there and possibly leading to conflict between groups of people.

In the chapters that follow, for the Palaeolithic and Mesolithic periods it is worth bearing in mind that the main focus of human occupation appears to have been on the Doggerland plains, and what was going on in Britain as a whole, as well as in our area, was inextricably linked to the events taking place in Doggerland.

Rediscovering Doggerland

Archaeologists have only just begun to investigate Doggerland, as being under as much as 120 metres of cold, stormy North Sea makes this challenging and research is at a very early, and exciting, phase.

The main sources of information about this lost land are found in the nets of fishing boats trawling the North Sea. Their giant nets scrape along the seabed and drag up everything they encounter. As well as the fish they seek, the trawlers regularly catch lumps of peat, the bones of ancient land animals and the stone, bone and antler tools of the human inhabitants of Doggerland. The first major discovery was a bone harpoon found embedded in a lump of peat caught in a net in the 1930s. By this time archaeologists were suspecting that what is now the North Sea may have been inhabited by prehistoric people, but this harpoon was the first proof that people had been there. Since that discovery, many more tools and a great number of animal bones have been recovered. Analysis of the pollen found in the peat has shown which trees and plants were present. The animal bones have included some surprises; bones of a sabre toothed cat have been found, dating to quite recent times, many thousands of years after this fearsome looking predator was believed to have become extinct.

As well as the finds from fishing nets, some underwater excavations have recently taken place in shallow coastal locations (mostly around Denmark, but some in British waters), revealing a number of drowned archaeological sites, including well preserved Mesolithic wooden structures, flint scatters and even human burials.

Other than this, proper archaeological exploration of the deeper parts of this lost land seems almost impossible. However, the North Sea has large reserves of oil and is a potential site for offshore wind farms, which has resulted in the seabed being studied in some detail, by methods such as sediment cores and geophysical survey. In a recent project by the University of Birmingham, the team examined some of the geophysical data for a small part of the North Sea. Amazingly, they were able to see the courses of ancient rivers and lakes, estuaries and salt marshes. They were even able to trace the history of some of the features. One massive lake on the Doggerland plain was inundated by the sea thousands of years ago, and the team were able to identify scouring which occurred when the sea rose and broke through into the lake, turning it into a saltwater estuary and an associated salt marsh.

It is becoming clear that an entire, preserved prehistoric country is awaiting exploration under the North Sea and that some of the techniques for investigating it are within our grasp.

Lower Palaeolithic

This chapter covers an immense length of time, a period of almost three quarters of a million years. It begins with the presence in the area that was later to become Britain of the earliest known human ancestors, as early as 1 million years ago, through several periods when these people abandoned the area and then returned, before ending at the start of the Devensian cold phase and the appearance of true Neanderthals around 60,000 years ago.

This vast period of time included glaciations during which it was so cold that the Midlands were covered by ice sheets over a mile in thickness. It also featured warm phases where hippopotamuses frolicked in the Trent and creatures that are now only found in Africa roamed the plains and forests of Britain, along with some gigantic species of animals which are now long extinct. The period also saw occupation by at least two different species of human ancestors. In the earlier phases (before the Anglian glaciation) Nottinghamshire would have been completely unrecognisable, but as the period progressed the features that define the modern landscape began to take shape.

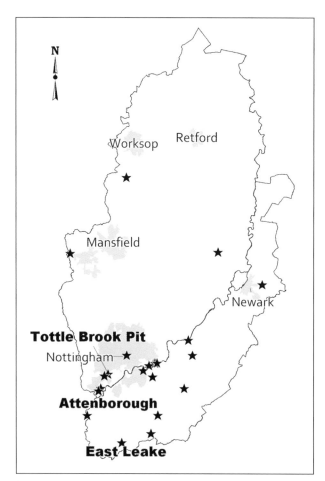

Lower Palaeolithic sites and finds in Nottinghamshire
Contains Ordnance Survey data © Crown copyright and database right 2011

The evidence from Nottinghamshire for this period is very limited and no in-situ sites are known. One reason for this was the Anglian glaciation, when ice over a mile thick covered the Midlands and swept the landscape clean of all traces of earlier activity. Later glaciations, while not necessarily burying the county under ice, resulted in the destruction of many sites due to massive remodelling caused by glacial outwash rivers. The result is that most very early finds from Nottinghamshire have come from river gravels, having been washed away from where they originally lay. They are in a rolled and battered condition, having been swept around in a river for possibly many thousands of years before being deposited in the gravels. Even so, the concentrations of flakes, tools and cores found in some locations suggest that the original sites may have been close to where the tools have ended up. Tottlebrook pit in Beeston in particular yielded a large collection of tools and flint waste. These were found early in the 20th century when gravel quarrying was mainly done by hand; increasing mechanisation of gravel extraction means that there is now much less chance of making such finds.

Tools, cores and waste flakes from Tottle Brook gravel pit, Beeston.
DJB/NCMG

Climate and Environment

The Lower Palaeolithic period covers such an immense period of time that the climate changed dramatically many times, with several cold periods interspersed with warm spells. Human activity in Britain was confined mostly to the warm phases, with people probably abandoning the area completely during the cold phases.

The warm phase which saw the earliest known occupation of Britain is part of the Cromerian Complex, named after the Cromer Forest Beds, a geological layer which has been found at various points along Britain's North Sea coast. The Cromer Forest Beds are in turn named after the quantities of fossil tree stumps found in them; they also contain a rich variety of animal bones, insect remains and plant material from a series of glacials and warm phases spanning about a quarter of a million years. Recent work on these deposits following the discovery of a scatter of worked flints has provided the earliest evidence for humans north of the Alps. The first finds are dated to around 700,000 years ago, and there are hints that there could have been early humans here up to 1 million years ago.

These early humans were present at times when the climate was a little warmer than today. The landscape in which they lived had a variety of habitats including oak woodland, open grassland and marshland, cut through by meandering rivers. This landscape was inhabited by a range of animals, some of which would be familiar today, such as horses, red deer and badgers, along with others such as rhinoceros, hippopotamus, bison, wolves, hyenas and lions. There were also a number of very unfamiliar creatures which are now long extinct. Some of these were of gigantic size, like the steppe mammoth (an ancestor of the woolly mammoth but considerably larger, standing up to 4.7m tall and with tusks up to 5m long), two species of giant deer, straight tusked elephant (about twice the size of a modern African elephant), a giant beaver and a species of sabre toothed cat.

A little after half a million years ago the Cromerian Complex ended with the dramatic cooling of the Anglian glaciation. This was the most extreme of the 'recent' glaciations and at its coldest ice over a mile thick covered the Midlands, the edge of the ice sheet advancing as far south as Bristol and London. The glaciers completely destroyed the landscape they covered, in places scouring the land surface down over 70 metres and in other places depositing large amounts of rock and clay which they had moved. They erased the Bytham river, which had been the main river flowing west to east and which provided the drainage for the Midlands and the East of England. It is likely to have been one of the major routes into Britain for early humans, and most of the pre-Anglian human activity is related to Bytham deposits. Following the Anglian glaciation the landscape began to take on a more familiar form, with rivers such as the Thames and the Trent taking up their modern courses.

This pattern of warm and cold phases was repeated several times, with animals and people moving back into Britain as the climate warmed and being pushed out again when it got cold. Britain was a north-western peninsula of Europe throughout most of the period, only briefly becoming an island during the very warmest phases.

Who were they?

It is not certain which species of human were the first to occupy Britain, up to a million years ago, as knowledge of this phase is so new and no human fossils have yet been discovered for this period. They were probably the species Homo Antecessor, known from sites in Spain around this time. The earliest known human remains from Britain belong to the species Homo heidelbergensis (the species was first identified by a professor at the University of Heidelberg). A shin bone from one individual and teeth from another have been discovered in pre-Anglian deposits, about half a million years old. Homo heidelbergensis was tall (around 1.80 metres, or 5 feet 11 inches) and very heavily built and the muscle attachments on their bones show they were very strong. Being tall and slender helps an organism to keep cool in hot climates, while being stocky is more of a cold climate adaptation, allowing the body to maintain heat. Because of this it seems they originally evolved in Africa but had begun to adapt to the colder climate of Europe. Their jaws were very heavy and powerful and had no chins. Aside from the lack of a chin, the most notable feature of their face would have been their extremely large and prominent brow ridges. They were mostly right handed and were quite long lived, individuals being known to survive into their 40s at least.

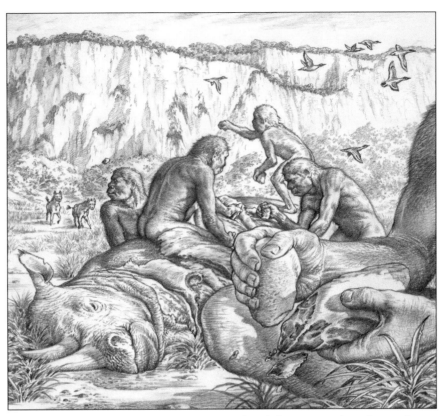

A group of Homo heidelbergensis butcher a rhino.
© *John Sibbick/The Natural History Museum, London*

Following the abandonment of Northern Europe during the cold of the Anglian glaciation a different species of human arrived to occupy Britain when temperatures rose again. These people are often known as 'pre-Neanderthals' since their fossil remains have many characteristics which can also be seen in the Neanderthals of the Middle Palaeolithic (see the next chapter). It is thought that these 'pre-Neanderthals' represent an intermediate step in the evolution of Homo heidelbergensis to Homo neanderthalis. In Britain remains of these people have been found at Swanscombe in Kent, where the rear part of a skull was discovered. They seem to have been the first to use fire and may even have practised some form of primitive burial rite.

Before Us - Early Human Minds

There is much debate about just how 'human' early humans were, whether they were capable of thought and reason or if they were merely glorified apes, human-shaped animals which had yet to develop any particular intelligence.

The production of handaxes suggests they could plan ahead. For a start, the stone for making handaxes was often obtained elsewhere and brought to the site for knapping. This shows that they recognised the raw material and realised that if they collected it, they would be able to use it to make a tool at some point in the future. Next is the actual production of the handaxe. To successfully produce a handaxe from a lump of flint you have to visualise the finished tool within the stone, and to cope with any flaws or problems that come up during the process. You cannot randomly start knapping and hope that by chance a handaxe pops out at the end! Soft hammers were used to make these tools, and an antler hammer found at Boxgrove showed extensive wear from sustained use, showing it had been used to make more than one handaxe. This suggests that they realised they might encounter a similar situation in future and kept tools which they knew might have further use.

Technology

350,000 year old handaxes from Camden, London and Hitchin, Herts. ©*Trustees of the British Museum*

Handaxes are the typical tool from this period. As the name suggests, they were made to be used just in bare hands, without being hafted. Compared to the finely worked oval or pointed types which are often illustrated in books, the handaxes from the Trent Valley look fairly crude and irregular. This is not because they were made by people who were less skilled; it is more to do with the available raw material. The flint nodules found in Nottinghamshire are not big enough to allow a knapper to make one of the standard handaxe shapes, so people made the best tool they could depending on the original size and shape of each nodule.

Apart from handaxes, sharp, unmodified flakes were also used for cutting. Flakes were also sometimes retouched, into scrapers. As well as flint they used quartzite which, unlike flint, is very common in Nottinghamshire.

A selection of handaxes from Tottle Brook gravel pit, Beeston. *DJB/NCMG*

In addition to stone tools, wood and antler were also used for making tools, for example a c.400,000 year old wooden spear was found at Clacton on Sea and a 500,000 year old antler 'soft hammer' for working flint at Boxgrove. Tools such as scrapers were used for preparing other materials such as hide, which has decayed away leaving no trace. We can only guess whether they made clothing.

Making a living

Evidence from a number of sites in Britain and on the continent tells us how these early humans were living. From cut marks and other damage to bones we know that they successfully hunted large game such as horses and also probably rhinoceros, bears and straight tusked elephants. From bone found at Boxgrove we know exactly how one particular hunt ended, 500,000 years ago. Homo heidelbergensis had brought down a horse, piercing it with their wooden spears. Damage to the animal's shoulder blade suggests that a spear hit it at relatively high speed, having been thrown from close range, rather than just being thrust at the horse when it was cornered or fallen. Once the animal was killed the hunters sat near the carcass and made some tools to butcher it. Armed with the handaxes they had just made, they began by skinning the horse. Once the skin was removed the animal was expertly dismembered, with the joints of meat and edible tissues carefully removed. Finally the long bones and some others were smashed open to obtain the nutritious marrow inside. When the hunters left the site, in addition to any equipment they arrived with and the meat, they also took the handaxes they had made. Cut marks in the skull suggest that the tongue and other soft tissues were removed and modern 'primitive' hunters do the same, eating the bone marrow, tongue and other perishable delicacies at the kill site, and then carrying the joints of meat back to camp to feed the tribe. The amount of meat on a horse could have fed a reasonable sized group of early humans for several weeks. Cut marks on human teeth from Boxgrove suggest that they cut their meat close to their mouths as they ate it, grabbing a mouthful between their teeth then cutting the piece away from the joint with a sharp flint. The Inuit still eat in a similar way today.

The fact that these people were able to kill animals such as horses, as well as very large and dangerous animals such as bears and even rhinos, shows that they were skilled hunters and masters of their environment. They could butcher the carcasses at leisure and even had time to extract marrow from bones, showing that they were able to keep other predators at bay for as long as they needed while they carried out their activities. Where bones show evidence of both carnivore and human activity, the cut marks of human activity always underlie the carnivore tooth marks. But there was probably a constant battle with packs of hyenas. These are very dangerous predators and were common throughout the Palaeolithic period; early humans probably spent a lot of energy keeping them at bay.

As well as hunting, people may have also scavenged carcasses which they found and in addition to meat, it is likely their diet included the edible plants, nuts and berries which were abundant in their surroundings. However, unlike stone and bone, plant material quickly decays and the traces left behind from obtaining and processing it are minimal, so archaeological proof remains elusive. People who live in modern day hunter-gatherer societies use all the resources they find around them and early humans no doubt did the same. On the other hand, recent chemical analysis of early human bones does seem to show that animal protein played a very important part in their diet, with plant material playing a minor role. The Boxgrove teeth have fairly heavy tartar deposits, more common in those with a diet high in animal protein. Also, in colder climates people will consume more meat as it provides a lot of energy and may simply be more easily available than other foods.

Housing

No structures are known and it is possible these early human species were not advanced enough to be capable of making shelters. They most likely slept in the open air, probably in the margins of forests where possible, as this would have been safer than sleeping on the open grassland.

Death and burial

Human skeletal material from this period is so rare that little can be said on this subject. A small section of shin bone from one individual from around 500,000 years ago and two teeth from another, earlier, individual, have been found at Boxgrove, while a fragment of skull from Swanscombe dates to around 400,000 years ago. There is no evidence of special treatment for the dead and no burials have been found.

The shin bone from Boxgrove was found on its own and had been gnawed by a carnivore (possibly a wolf) but it is not known if this individual was killed by animals or if, once dead, the body was taken by scavengers.

Towards the end of the Lower Palaeolithic there was a lengthy period when it appears that no humans set foot in Britain for around 100,000 years. This was followed by the Devensian cold phase, as conditions in Britain became similar to those in arctic tundra today. Animals and early humans had to adapt to the new, harsher environment and the presence of a new species of human marks the change to the Middle Palaeolithic period.

Middle Palaeolithic

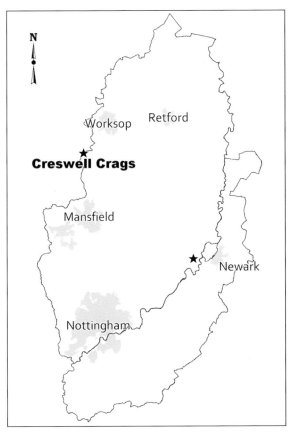

Middle Palaeolithic sites and finds in Nottinghamshire
Contains Ordnance Survey data © Crown copyright and database right 2011

The Middle Palaeolithic period is the first time when we can identify the actual sites of human activity in Nottinghamshire, with artefacts found where they were used and discarded tens of thousands of years ago. These few artefacts relate to the activities of Neanderthals during the early part of the Devensian cold phase, which began around 60,000 years ago.

Some important traces from this period have come from Creswell Crags, a limestone gorge straddling the Derbyshire / Nottinghamshire border. In the walls of the crags are a series of caves and fissures which contained an absolute treasure trove of remains from the Ice Age, starting from the Middle Palaeolithic period.

Creswell Crags.
DJB

Climate and Environment

The Devensian cold phase was, as the name suggests, cooler than today. On the whole, conditions were similar to those of the arctic tundra today, with braided rivers and few trees, populated by cold adapted animals, including mammoths, woolly rhinos, wild horses, hyenas, bears and wolves. Sea levels were low, and Britain was a peninsula at the north-western edge of Doggerland.

Mammoth steppe, with typical animals of this habitat.
Mauricio Anton/Creative Commons

Who were they?

The people inhabiting the land during this period (and probably into the early Upper Palaeolithic) were a new type of human, the Neanderthals. This species is named after the Neander Valley in Germany, where

Reconstructed face of a Neanderthal.
© *Robert Laws/The Natural History Museum, London*

the first specimen to be described scientifically was found during quarrying in the 1850s. They survived and flourished over a wide geographical range and for a great length of time, in fact inhabiting the planet for a considerably longer period than we modern humans have so far managed. They were native Europeans, having evolved here from Homo heidelbergensis.

There is a lot of academic argument about the Neanderthals, over how similar or how different to us they were, and what happened to Neanderthals when modern humans arrived. As more Neanderthal bones have been found and studied, our knowledge of them has increased and we can say more about them. Their bodies were very robustly built and they were generally not as tall as modern humans, with short, powerful arms and legs. They had strong jaws and very prominent brow ridges, but recessed chins. Their squat physique suggests that they had evolved to thrive in cold conditions. Their broad flat noses may have helped to warm inhaled air or to aid cooling after strenuous activity. Wear patterns on teeth suggest that they used their jaws for more than just chewing food, perhaps to hold things they were working on, or to soften animal hides by chewing for use in clothing. Faint cut marks on their teeth suggest they cut meat close to the mouth, as their ancestors did in the Lower Palaeolithic. These marks also suggest they were mostly right handed. Muscle attachments on their bones show they were stronger than modern humans. Certain small bones found in the area of the voice box indicate that they were physically capable of speech, though it is not known whether they had language. They did not live as long as modern humans, generally dying in their 30s. Neanderthal children also matured more quickly than modern human children do. Now efforts are being made to produce a genome sequence for the Neanderthals and there are already hints that there was interbreeding between them and modern humans, who first arrived in the Upper Palaeolithic.

Technology

Middle Palaeolithc assemblage from Creswell Crags, made using a variety of locally available raw materials.
DJB/DMG/NCMG

Handaxes were still produced during this period, as well as a range of simple flakes which were used for cutting or were retouched into large scrapers. Local materials were used, including quartzite cobbles and clay ironstone. The few flint tools of this period from Creswell were probably brought to the site from some distance away as flint is hard to find locally. The tiny handaxe (top right in above illustration) made of flint shows that even when only small nodules of flint were available, handaxes were still the preferred tool.

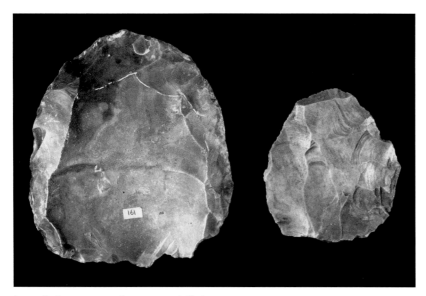

Neanderthals also used a technology (known as prepared core technology, or Levallois, after the suburb of Paris where it was first recognised) which gave more control over the shape of the flakes produced. This technique was used to produce flakes and blades and was particularly used for making 'Mousterian points', triangular points which were hafted as spear tips.

Levallois prepared core and flake.
©*Trustees of the British Museum*

Making a living

The reappearance of humans in Britain during this period, after an absence of around 100,000 years, came at a time of cold, tundra-type conditions and cold-adapted animals. It seems that the Neanderthals moved into Britain following the herds of mammoths, woolly rhinos, wild horses and reindeer which were their food and which wandered freely across Doggerland.

The Neanderthals' stocky build, robust skeleton and powerful muscles meant they were capable of delivering sudden bursts of speed along with very powerful spear thrusts and throws. Many Neanderthal skeletons show a range of injuries similar to those sustained by rodeo riders today, suggesting they used this speed and strength to attack large animals at close range. Given the size of their prey this must have been a risky business. However some sites show that their hunting was not always about brute force and speed. At Cotte de St Brelade on what is now the island of Jersey, Neanderthals managed to drive a herd of mammoths over a cliff, causing them to fall to their deaths. This must have required the close co-operation of many individuals. At this particular site, the technique was used on at least two separate occasions and the tools used to butcher the dead mammoths were found scattered around the skeletons.

There are only a few sites of this period in Britain, and the number of finds from each site is minimal. At Creswell Crags, a small but significant assemblage of stone tools and debris has been found which was preserved after being washed into the caves from the activity areas in the cave mouth. It seems that this material was left by small groups of people who made a number of visits on different occasions, stopping only for a short time during each visit, perhaps using the gorge to shelter in overnight while out on hunting trips following large animals which were passing through the area. During their visits they ate (reindeer on one occasion, as reindeer leg bones with cut marks were found here), repaired their toolkits, prepared hides or worked wood and made new tools from raw materials they had picked up in the area. When they moved on, presumably as the herds did, they took most of their new tools with them and left behind small quantities of waste flakes and a few abandoned tools.

Housing

No structures have yet been found which can be attributed to Neanderthals. They used caves and rock shelters when they were available but probably slept in the open elsewhere, though the prevailing cold conditions suggest they may have needed some kind of shelter or furs for blankets when camping away from caves.

Death and Burial

No Neanderthal burials have been found in Britain and only one possible fragment of Neanderthal bone has been discovered here so far, but in other places where they lived there are examples of Neanderthals having been buried in graves and even with grave goods, the very first signs of ritual behaviour. They are found laid on their side with their arms and legs drawn into the body, as though sleeping (known as a crouched inhumation). Sometimes a few stone tools and animal bones are found with them; however, there may also have been perishable items since pollen from a Neanderthal burial in the Middle East suggests the person was laid to rest with many flowers, some now known to have medicinal properties.

Altogether there is very little evidence for life in Britain in the Middle Palaeolithic period, but the picture we have so far suggests small scale activity at sites which were occupied for only short periods of time by groups of Neanderthals who occasionally passed through the area, living right at the edge of the range of their species. Life continued in much the same way for the next 20 to 30,000 years with Neanderthal hunters continuing to follow the herds across the steppe, until major change came around 40,000 years ago with the arrival of modern humans in the final part of the Palaeolithic period.

Upper Palaeolithic

The Upper Palaeolithic period saw the arrival of the first modern humans in Europe. They brought with them new technologies and the first flowering of art as we would recognise it. This period also saw the extinction of our closest ancestor, the Neanderthals.

A severe cold phase, the last glacial maximum, divided the early Upper Palaeolithic (about 40,000 to 22,000 years ago) from the late Upper Palaeolithic (13,000 to 10,000 years ago). During the late glacial maximum temperatures dropped so low that no human set foot in Britain for almost 10,000 years, as the people and many of the animals moved south to warmer places like the south of France. The Upper Palaeolithic in turn ended with a sudden intense period of cold, known as the Younger Dryas, at about 11,000 years ago. Once again, the cold forced the people to move to warmer areas in Europe.

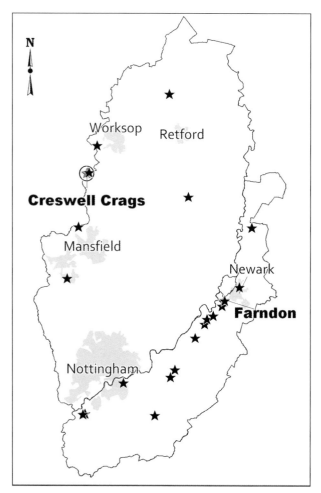

Upper Palaeolithic sites and finds in Nottinghamshire
○ = early Upper Palaeolithic
★ = late Upper Palaeolithic
Contains Ordnance Survey data © Crown copyright and database right 2011

During the Upper Palaeolithic period it seems that people mostly lived in small groups, moving across large areas from the plains of Doggerland up into the highlands of Britain and out into mainland Europe. We can compare British sites of the period to those which are now on the other side of the Channel, since the same groups could easily have visited all these areas during their lives.

Though early Upper Palaeolithic sites are extremely rare and late Upper Palaeolithic sites are not at all common in Britain, a number of them have been found in Nottinghamshire. This is even more surprising considering that, due to the cold, Nottinghamshire was about the most north-westerly point in Europe where habitation was possible at some points during this period. The caves at Creswell Crags have long been known to contain some of Britain's most important Palaeolithic remains, but recently they have risen to international fame with the discovery of the country's only cave art from this period. In addition, recent work on the route of the A46 road has discovered an important late Upper Palaeolithic site at Farndon near Newark.

Climate and Environment

The climate varied dramatically throughout this period, alternating between periods of extreme cold and temperatures similar to today. There were several periods of intense cold when people were entirely absent from Britain. As in the previous Middle Palaeolithic period, conditions were mostly what is known as "mammoth steppe". Hyenas, woolly rhinos, wild horses, woolly mammoths, wolverines, aurochs (huge wild cattle), giant deer, wolves, red deer, brown bears, mountain hares, arctic foxes and reindeer were present and the bones of lions have even been found at Creswell. However, following the last glacial maximum a number of species, many of which had been present for hundreds of thousands of years, did not return as temperatures rose again in the late Upper Palaeolithic. These included bison, woolly rhinos and lions, but most welcome for man must have been the absence of hyenas, after thousands of years of conflict.

As a result of the generally cold conditions, sea levels remained low. The Trent was an important route from the Doggerland plain and provided a range of resources to be exploited. It was probably also an important part of the migration route of certain animals such as reindeer which moved seasonally from the lowland plains of Doggerland to the uplands of the Derbyshire peaks to calve in safety. Rivers were generally braided, with a network of active and abandoned shallow channels spreading across wide floodplains.

Who were they?

The early Upper Palaeolithic period saw the demise of the Neanderthals and the appearance of modern humans in Britain, though for maybe 3,000 years both species might have been present here together. There are sites where we are not sure whether the archaeological remains were left by the first modern humans or the last Neanderthals.

Modern humans from this time are known as Cro-Magnons, after the French site where they were first recognised, dating from around 40,000 years ago. Compared to the Neanderthals they were tall and slender, a body shape which suggests that they were adapted to living in warm climates and supports the idea that they evolved in Africa before dispersing to Europe. They were practically identical to us - a Cro-Magnon could walk down any street in the modern world and not get a second glance. Even their life expectancy was similar to that of people living today. Unlike the Neanderthals, Cro-Magnons are known to have lived into their 50s.

As modern humans became established Neanderthals began to disappear from their old habitats, finally becoming extinct in Europe between 28,000 and 24,000 years ago. It seems that they were finished off by the combination of two factors: changes in the climate and competition from modern humans. However, studies of Neanderthal DNA are just beginning and there are hints that some interbreeding with modern humans took place.

Technology

In terms of stone tools, the Upper Palaeolithic period was the era of the blade. This new way of working stone totally swept away the ancient traditions of handaxes and core tools which had lasted for thousands of years. Instead of chipping away at a nodule to shape a single tool or carefully preparing a core in order to strike off one or two flakes of a particular shape, knappers could now produce blade after blade of consistent shape from each core, every blade having the potential to be made into a tool.

Another reason for the change may have been because now many tools were set into wooden handles. It is far quicker and 'cheaper' to make a stone tool, in terms of effort, than it is to make the wooden handle to hold it. Once a stone blade became blunt or broken through use it could easily be replaced with another, since with blade technology it is very easy to make a replacement of the same shape and size.

As well as the use of blades, the Upper Palaeolithic period saw an increase in the types of stone tools being made along with an explosion in the working of organic materials. Of the stone tools, burins, used for working antler and bone, became common, along with piercers and borers, for making holes in hide and drilling holes in wood, bone or antler.

Early Upper Palaeolithic
The oldest of the early Upper Palaeolithic cultures in Britain produced 'leaf points' such as these from Creswell Crags, around 40,000 years ago. These points were usually made on triangular sectioned blades which were retouched at both ends to give them their leaf shape. The retouch also thinned the butt end to

make them easier to haft. A number of examples have been found which show damage caused by impact, so it seems they were used as spear points. In areas where large nodules of good quality flint are not easy to find, the bases of leaf points broken in use were often re-worked into other tools such as scrapers or burins.

Three blade points from Creswell Crags.
These were probably used as spear points.
DJB/DMG/NCMG/CHT

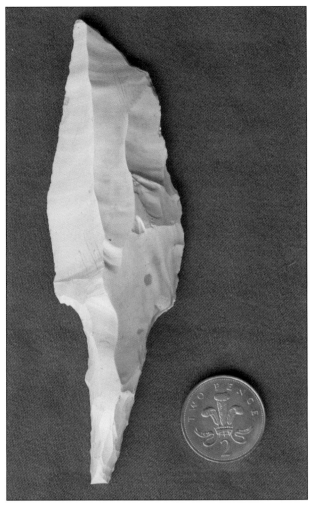

A Gravettian tanged point from Creswell Crags, made around 28,000 years ago. It was probably hafted and used as a knife.
DJB/UM/CHT

Penknife point from Creswell Crags.
DJB/CHT

The last culture of the early Upper Palaeolithic period is definitely the work of modern humans rather than Neanderthals. Their culture is known as the Gravettian and their defining tools were tanged points. A tang is the slender extension of the object which allows the tool to be securely attached to a handle (this design is still in widespread use today for a wide variety of tools such as knives, chisels and files). Although they are called points, traces of wear on similar tools from Europe suggest that they were used as knives, not weapon tips. Sites of this period are incredibly rare in Britain, with just eight currently known in the whole country. Of the 10 tanged points found in Britain, two were found at Creswell Crags, dating from around 28,000 years ago.

Late Upper Palaeolithic

The first culture to appear in Britain after the late glacial maximum was the Creswellian, named after Creswell Crags. It is similar to the Magdalenian culture of France and the southern parts of Europe and in Britain it lasted from around 12,600 to around 12,000 years ago. There are only around 30 Creswellian sites currently known in Britain.

The Creswellian was followed (and perhaps overlapped) by a culture which has similarities to industries in Germany and the Low Countries, and lasted from about 12,000 to 11,500 years ago. This culture is sometimes called "Federmesser", after a diagnostic tool which looks a bit like a pen-knife (the German for pen-knife is Federmesser). Sites of this type are much more numerous than Creswellian ones, though their assemblages look very similar, with a few differences in the way knapping was carried out and in the design of certain points.

Making a living

Early Upper Palaeolithic

There is little that can be said about how people were living during the early Upper Palaeolithic period. This is because most sites of this date in Britain consist of just a handful of artefacts left by scarce and highly mobile groups stopping only for short periods of time. However, certain key sites provide some clues, letting us glimpse the daily lives of the people who were probably the last Neanderthals in Britain.

At Beedings in Suffolk a camp of leaf point users was discovered. Here, on a high ridge overlooking a river valley, a hunting party settled down to repair their equipment. Spearheads broken during the hunt were removed from their wooden shafts and repaired or replaced. Many broken points with fractures characteristic of impact damage were found but the tips were missing, lost at the kill site which was probably somewhere down in the valley. As the area had very little in the way of flint resources the broken points were recycled and used as raw material to make a variety of other tools such as scrapers, burins and borers, presumably to process the day's kills. Choosing to camp on a locally high point meant the hunters had good views of the surrounding land and could track the movements of animals below, planning the next hunting trip while repairing their equipment and resting.

Another temporary camp of this period was discovered at Glaston in Leicestershire. Here a leaf point was found along with a core and a number of flakes, some of which had been retouched into tools. This again represents a short stay by a small group, probably on a hunting trip.

In Nottinghamshire the evidence paints a similar picture. Around 20 leaf points have been found at Creswell, suggesting that the caves provided temporary shelter for groups of hunters passing through the area. They probably returned to Creswell several times, to intercept animals migrating through the gorge.

Right at the end of the early Upper Palaeolithic period we get the first indications that there was more to life than just hunting. Around 28,000 or 29,000 years ago, a group of people ventured into the north-western peninsula on an expedition looking for mammoth ivory. They stopped off in the shelter of Paviland cave in Wales to work the ivory into rods, which were probably blanks for beads or other ornaments, and rings. While they were on this expedition one of the party died. Study of his bones has shown that, in addition to eating large game animals, they may have been some of the first fishermen. His diet consisted of around 20% fish, which contrasts with the earlier Neanderthals who apparently ate only meat from the large game that they hunted.

Late Upper Palaeolithic

There is much more evidence for all aspects of life in the late Upper Palaeolithic period. At this time, grassland and birch woodland supported a wide range of game animals, including woolly mammoths, wild horses, red deer, aurochs and arctic hares. Also present were brown bears and wolves. Many of these species were hunted for food and their bones have been found at Creswell Crags. Depictions of red deer and an aurochs or bison in the Creswell cave art, along with the engraving of a wild horse on a piece of rib bone testify to the importance of these species to the people. The animals were not hunted just for food. In addition to its meat, an animal would provide skins for clothing and tent coverings, antlers and horns for making tools, bone which not only provided nutritious marrow but also could be made into tools, tendons which could be dried and used as thread, teeth for pendants and maybe even hooves to be rendered into glue.

Engraved image of a horse on a rib bone, from Creswell Crags.
©Trustees of the British Museum

The Przewalski horse is the closest living relative to the wild horses of the last Ice Age.
©iStockphoto.com/rhabdias

As with all humans throughout the Upper Palaeolithic period, Creswellian groups appear to have been highly mobile, moving through very large territories, following the seasonal movements of game. Their closest cultural links are found in France, suggesting they either had long distance contacts or that their seasonal movements took them all the way across Doggerland, between what is now France and Britain. Some animals depicted in cave art were not native to the area where the art was created and could only have been encountered hundreds of miles away, suggesting that the artist had travelled over very long distances. However, the distinctive Creswell points made during this period only occur in Britain and so seem to indicate a regional aspect of the culture.

An elaborately carved spear-thrower in the shape of a mammoth, from Montastruc, France.
©*Trustees of the British Museum*

The main tool used for hunting at this time was the spear. A new development was the spear-thrower, made of antler or bone, which increased the force (and consequently the range and killing power) with which a person could launch a spear. This also allowed people to stand further away from aggressive or wounded animals, lessening the risk of being injured themselves. Some spear-throwers are very highly decorated, and they must have been valued objects.

The spear was not the only means of obtaining food and clothing. One of the Creswell caves was used by hunters who were out trapping arctic hares, using snares. At the entrance to the cave they processed the pelts and were sewing them together. Many awls (a sharp, needle like tool used for piercing holes in skins) made of hare bone were found, along with needles and flint scrapers. The winter coat of the arctic hare is warm and soft and a brilliant white and was probably highly prized.

Whether the Creswellian occupation of Britain represents visits of groups of hunters coming up from France, distinct groups from Doggerland or local groups in residence, it seems they returned to certain places in the landscape time and again. At Farndon, near Newark, a late Upper Palaeolithic flint scatter was discovered, at the confluence of the rivers Trent and Devon. It appears that this was a crossing point used by migrating animals, which are at their most vulnerable and easiest to pick off when crossing rivers. The size of the scatter is probably the result of repeated visits as people returned year after year to ambush the herds they knew would cross here. Creswell Crags also shows signs of multiple visits and the cave art could have been produced as a guide to what the area had to offer for later visits or for other hunters coming into the area.

Although sites of the later Federmesser culture are more common in Britain, we actually know less about how the people were living, as, unlike the Creswellian culture, they did not produce rich artwork or highly decorated equipment.

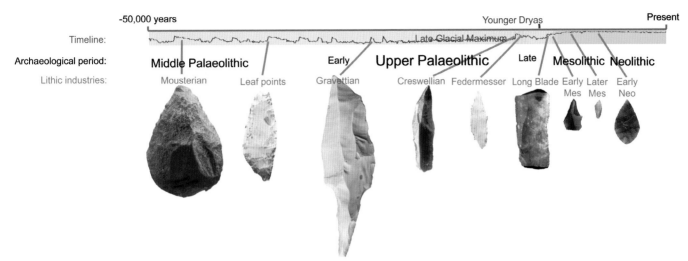

Timeline:
-50,000 years
Younger Dryas
Late Glacial Maximum
Present

Archaeological period:
Middle Palaeolithic
Early **Upper Palaeolithic** Late **Mesolithic Neolithic**

Lithic industries:
Mousterian
Leaf points
Gravettian
Creswellian
Federmesser
Long Blade
Early Mes
Later Mes
Early Neo

Timeline of the last 50,000 years, with characteristic
tools of the main cultural groupings
DJB/UM/DMG/NCMG/CHT/GG

Neanderthal hunters tackle a woolly rhino.
© Dominic Andrews: www.archaeoart.co.uk

Engravings from Creswell Crags

The bird and the aurochs or bison have been digitally enhanced to make them easier to see.

Stag *DJB/CHT*

Bird (possibly a curlew)
DJB/CHT

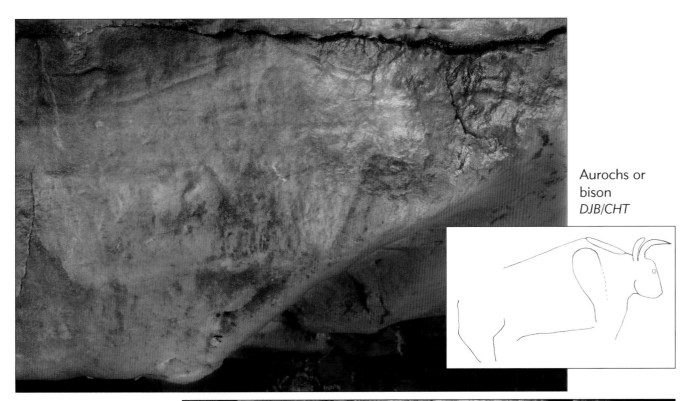

Aurochs or
bison
DJB/CHT

Unknown
(perhaps birds ?)
DJB/CHT

Mesolithic painted pebbles from Mas d'Azil, France. ©*Trustees of the British Museum*

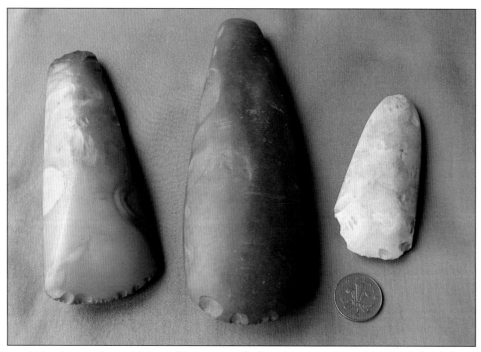

Neolithic polished axes from Holme Pierrepont (left and centre) and Bulwell (right). *DJB/NCMG*

Housing

Caves provided shelter throughout the Upper Palaeolithic period. At Creswell the late Upper Palaeolithic people preferred to camp on the south facing side of the gorge as this side received more sunlight and so was warmer than the opposite side. They also camped in open air locations and it is from the Upper Palaeolithic period that the first evidence of structures built by humans is found. On the continent the remains of various types of houses have been found. Some of the earliest, from eastern Europe, were substantial structures built using mammoth bone and tusks to construct circular huts, which were then covered with mammoth hide. During the late Upper Palaeolithic period free standing tents and lean-tos erected against rock faces were built. These had a structure of wood or possibly mammoth tusk and were covered with skins, which were often weighted down at the bottom of the structure using rocks or antler. No such structures have yet been found in Britain but this is probably because so few Upper Palaeolithic open air sites have ever been properly investigated.

Death and burial

The oldest formal burial of a modern human in Britain, and indeed the oldest in western Europe, is that of the 'Red Lady of Paviland'. This was a skeleton found in Paviland cave in South Wales in the early 19th century. The individual was buried with a mammoth skull and many ivory beads and periwinkle shells which were pierced for sewing on to clothing. It was also completely covered in red ochre. The original excavator suggested it was of a Roman, and due to the presence of the beads and the shells he assumed it must have been a female, with the red ochre suggesting to him that she was a prostitute associated with a nearby Roman camp.

However, the burial is actually that of an adult male who was laid to rest around 29,000 years ago, not that long before the last glacial maximum at the end of the early Upper Palaeolithic period wiped out all human activity here. Unlike earlier Neanderthal burials from Europe, he was buried extended and was accompanied with a variety of grave goods. Some of these were part of the clothes he wore from day to day, such as the pierced shells and beads made of mammoth ivory, while others were probably deposited in the grave as goods to accompany the deceased. These included the mammoth skull and unfinished mammoth ivory rods which were probably blanks for beads, perhaps being made by this man but not finished before he died.

This contrasts with the treatment of a group of late Upper Palaeolithic people found in the Cheddar Gorge in Somerset. Here the human remains bore cut marks made by flint tools, showing that the bodies had been dismembered and defleshed in the same way that prey animals were processed. This may be evidence of cannibalism. However, this has also been a standard funerary practice in some cultures, so it need not mean that people were killing and eating each other.

Art

The Upper Palaeolithic period saw an astonishing flowering of art in Europe. No art is known from the hundreds of thousands of years of human existence before this and nothing comparable is known from the following periods of prehistory. It could even be argued that the techniques used by Palaeolithic artists to show movement and perspective were not bettered until the Renaissance, 10,000 years later. The oldest of the painted caves in Europe date from the same time as the arrival of fully modern humans, in the early Upper Palaeolithic period. The sophisticated artistic tradition of cave painting, mobile artwork and carved statuettes, along with technically advanced use of antler, bone and ivory for tools as well as decorative objects, marks a major difference between modern humans and the Neanderthals.

The art takes many forms. Paintings, engravings and sculpture are found on the walls, floors and ceilings of caves (such as the world famous caves of Lascaux, Altamira and Chauvet). The subjects chosen by the artists were wide ranging. Much of the art shows the animals which would have been of greatest importance to these nomadic people who survived by hunting and gathering, so representations of their main quarry such as red deer, reindeer, horse, mammoth, bison and ibex are common. Rarer are images of the more dangerous carnivores like bears and lions, which would have been in competition with the humans for food and may well have preyed upon unwary people. Representations of people are rare, though outlines of hand prints are found. These were created by placing the hand on the wall, then blowing or spitting pigment at it, and when the hand was removed from the wall this left the shape outlined in paint. As well as images of things found in the real world, the Palaeolithic artists also drew things from their imagination, such as beasts created by combining different types of real animal, and half human-half animal creatures. They also drew a variety of geometric shapes.

Most of the art so far discovered has been found in caves and rock shelters, because these provide a very stable environment which protects the contents. It is probable that much more art was created in the open air than in caves, but paintings or engravings done outside will have been quite quickly eroded away by the weather. What is known as 'portable art' is also found. This includes engravings on small pieces of stone, bone, antler and ivory, along with carvings and sculpture made of similar materials and even fired clay, which is the first pottery ever produced. Subject matter was similar to that of the cave art, often depicting animals, but there are rather more human forms, including female figurines which have been interpreted as "mother goddesses" and some half human, half animal creatures.

Very little Palaeolithic art is known from Britain and most of it comes from Creswell Crags. Over many years of excavation the site had produced two pieces of portable art. Recently, against all expectation, the first ice age cave art from the whole of Britain was discovered here.

The art is engraved rather than painted and modern graffiti and erosion has obscured some of it, but clearly visible are a stag and an aurochs or bison. Elsewhere, other creatures are represented including horses and birds, along with a number of strange triangles and sinuous lines. Natural shapes in the cave walls and ceilings are incorporated as part of the images. (See colour plates, pages 35 and 36)

Cave art was not confirmed as being Palaeolithic in date until the close of the 19th century, when excavation in a French cave discovered paintings in a gallery that had previously been blocked off by sediments containing Palaeolithic tools. Since then, scientific methods have allowed much more precise dating. Radiocarbon dating on charcoal used in the paint has proved that the fabulous paintings at Chauvet cave are the oldest known paintings in the world at around 32,000 years ago. Dating the Creswell art was more difficult as it is engraved into the rock, so no carbon could be tested. The carvings were obviously old due to the weathering of the engraved lines, and they are stylistically very similar to known ice age art. Luckily, parts of the engravings are covered with a stalactite-like deposit which could be dated. This proved that the deposit had formed over the surface of the engravings around 12,000 years ago and that the carvings must therefore be older than this, confirming the dating based on their style.

What does it mean?

It is difficult to know what art meant to Palaeolithic people. Study of modern hunter-gatherers suggests that it may have had some form of magical purpose. For example, a horse engraved into a spear thrower might have been intended to lend the swiftness of the horse to the spear. The images of animals on cave walls could have been created to bring them near, to increase their numbers, or to magically aid the hunters to make them more successful in the hunt.

There is tantalising evidence that cave art was created for ritual purposes. Cave paintings are usually found deep within caves, far beyond the reach of natural light (some paintings are more than half a kilometre underground) and could only have been made and viewed with the help of lamps or torches. The chambers in which the paintings are found also often have very good acoustics, suggesting that sound may have played an important role in whatever ritual was taking place. Engravings, on the other hand, tend to be found in places where natural light can reach. At Creswell, study of the engravings has revealed that they show up best in natural light and must have been created to be viewed that way, not by torch light. Interestingly, the richest art at Creswell is found in a cave with very little evidence of occupation. It seems that the hunters using the gorge preferred to camp on the south-facing side of the gorge, where there was more sunlight and warmth, but created their art in caves on the shadowy, mysterious side.

Many of the engravings at Creswell are interpreted as representing stylised parts of the female anatomy. These may have been for ritual purposes, maybe used in fertility rites. Alternatively, were they actually just the product of a hunting party camping in the gorge and missing their women?

Another explanation for cave art is that it was a way of telling others coming into an area what sort of resources that area had to offer (in the case of Creswell, red deer, bison and horses). In some of the caves on the continent large numbers of predators such as lions were drawn, and this could be a warning to keep a sharp eye out.

Some recent and exciting research has suggested that the geometric patterns (e.g. circles, crosses, lines and dots) which are frequently found in cave art may be some kind of symbolic communication. Certain signs appear again and again, drawn the same way each time. This suggests that they were meant to convey some kind of meaning.

Right at the end of the Upper Palaeolithic period the cold of the Younger Dryas again drove humans out of Britain. When people returned as the temperatures rose after about 10,200 years ago, they were part of a culture which is also seen in Germany, Holland and Belgium. The technology they used was based around production of very long blades. Less than 30 sites of this period are known in Britain and most of these are in the south of the country. However, recent discoveries of long blade sites at Ockbrook in Derbyshire and Launde in Leicestershire show that these people were present in the Midlands. Their technology was mostly Upper Palaeolithic in character (with the production of large blades), but also had elements which anticipated the technologies of the Mesolithic which was to follow.

They were also the first people in Western Doggerland known to have used the bow and arrow. At Stellmoor in Germany, excavation investigated a site where a group of hunters had ambushed reindeer which were swimming across a lake on their annual migration. Preserved in the lake mud were hundreds of wooden arrows and several bows. Analysis of the wounds on the reindeer bones prove they were attacked while swimming and the mud of the former lake bed even preserved the droppings of the terrified and dying animals.

These were the last people of the Ice Age, and their world was changing around them. Temperatures continued to increase, causing sea levels to rise as the ice melted. Huge areas of land were drowned, and the climate and vegetation were also changing, to become similar to conditions we live in today. This was the end of the Palaeolithic period and the beginning of the Mesolithic period.

Mesolithic

The Mesolithic period was the start of the warm phase we live in today, and it marks the end of the Pleistocene era and the beginning of the Holocene. It covers a period of around 4,000 years, during which the most dramatic changes in the geography and environment of Britain ever seen by modern humans took place. Sea levels rose due to melting ice, from around 55 metres below the current level at the end of the Younger Dryas cold phase to modern levels by around 7,500 years ago. This resulted in the loss of the rich habitats of Doggerland, the heartlands of the Mesolithic people. Britain became an island separated from Europe.

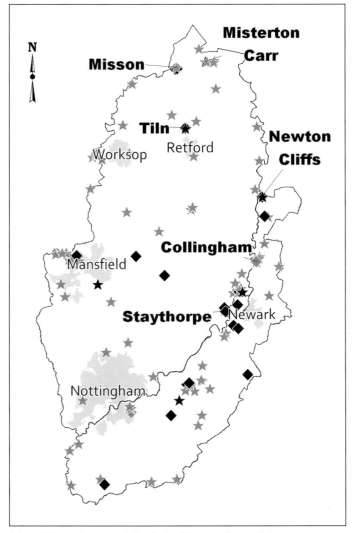

Mesolithic sites and finds in Nottinghamshire
★ = Mesolithic (unspecified)
★ = earlier Mesolithic
◆ = later Mesolithic
Contains Ordnance Survey data © Crown copyright and database right 2011

This period is divided into earlier and later phases, based on changes in material culture. In the early Mesolithic (from about 9,700 to 8,650 years ago) the occupants of Britain were part of a culture which stretched across much of Europe, from Britain through Doggerland to northern France, northern Germany, Sweden, Denmark and the Low Countries. During the later Mesolithic (from about 8,650 to 5,500 years ago), as sea levels rose and Britain became increasingly geographically isolated, the people here began to develop new technologies which were different from those on the continent. The Mesolithic also saw the beginning of continuous human occupation of Britain which continues to this day.

Mesolithic sites are rare and often all that is found are scatters of flint tools. For this reason, a lot of our information comes from just a few sites where preservation is better. At Star Carr in Yorkshire waterlogged conditions preserved a remarkable array of structures and objects of wood and bone, giving us a unique window into life at this time. In Nottinghamshire, traces of Mesolithic settlement are often found on high ground or promontories near to water, and there are concentrations of sites in the low lying carr lands in the north of the county and a number of sites along the Trent Valley.

Climate and Environment

Early successional landscape at Steetley quarry. This sort of environment might have been encountered shortly after the ice melted.
NC

The warming that began about 10,000 years ago lasted no more than a few generations, with temperatures rising dramatically from the intense cold of the Younger Dryas to levels similar to those of today in as little as 50 years. The open tundra of the Palaeolithic period gave way to extensive forest cover as trees re-colonised the land, spreading from the sheltered valleys in the south where they had clung to survival throughout the coldest parts of the ice ages. The first colonisers were birch and pine, with hazel and elm following shortly afterwards.

Gradually, pine gave way to other species and mixed deciduous woodlands of oak, elder, lime, ash and hazel became established in the later Mesolithic.

Melting ice meant that large volumes of water flowed down the rivers, causing them to cut deeply into their floodplains. Vegetation growing on the banks helped to stabilise the channels. Floodplains were wide, with one or more active channels winding their way along and a network of abandoned river beds and cut-off meanders in various states of silting up.

Birch forest in Sherwood Forest National Nature Reserve
NC

The newly wooded landscape was not at all suitable for the great herds of animals which had roamed the tundra of the Palaeolithic period and which the hunters had depended upon. Reindeer need an open environment and avoided the advancing forests, following the retreating ice northwards and eventually arriving at their current ranges in Siberia, Norway, Greenland, Alaska and Canada. Wild horses also dislike wooded environments and they died out in Britain, whilst surviving on the continent. Other large animals which had been part of the landscape for hundreds of thousands of years were not so lucky. Both the woolly mammoth and giant deer became extinct around the start of the Holocene. While the changing climate played its part, overexploitation by humans was probably the factor which pushed them over the edge.

Other species thrived in the new woodland, including red deer, roe deer, wild boar, aurochs and elk, occupying the forests all year round. More species of plants were now available in the forests, including many which produced edible tubers, nuts and berries.

Who were they?

The people of the Mesolithic period were totally modern humans. The only difference is that in modern times people tend to be taller, due to improved nutrition; analysis of the (very rare) Mesolithic human bones from Britain, along with tracks of footprints have shown that larger individuals (assumed to be male) stood an average of 1.65 metres (5 feet 5 inches) tall, with smaller individuals (assumed to be female) at an average of 1.45 metres (4 feet 9 inches).

Mesolithic human footprints have been found in several places around the British coast, preserved in mud which hardened soon after people had passed by. As well as providing direct evidence of people moving across the landscape, they also preserve some very familiar behaviour. One set of tracks was left by an adult who was crossing the mud, followed by a child who walked in its parent's footprints, leaping from one to the next and not straying onto virgin mud.

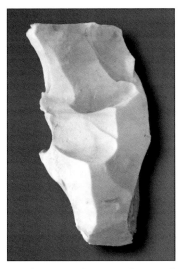

Possible evidence for the teaching of children was revealed at Coulerach in Scotland, where spreads of flint waste show where an experienced knapper was sitting making tools. Sitting nearby was another knapper, whose output was nowhere near as competent. This was likely to have been a child watching an adult working flint and trying to copy what they saw. An early Mesolithic blade core found at Misterton in Nottinghamshire appears to have been made by a very incompetent knapper who made a variety of mistakes, resulting in a number of "hinge fractures", where the flake comes off part way down the core, leaving a thick "hinged" scar. An experienced knapper could have fixed this but this person just kept on trying. Again, maybe this was a child making their first attempts at knapping.

Blade core showing hinge fractures, possibly the work of a trainee knapper. From Misterton Carr.
DJB/DOM

Technology

In the Mesolithic period, as at the end of the Palaeolithic period, the main aim of knapping was the careful production of blades, though these tend to be smaller than the Palaeolithic examples and got smaller still in the later Mesolithic period. These blades were then worked into very small tools known as microliths. Microliths are the diagnostic tool type of the Mesolithic period. They were made so that several could be stuck into a shaft or handle, using pine or birch resin as a glue, to make composite tools such as barbed arrows, harpoons and knives with long cutting edges.

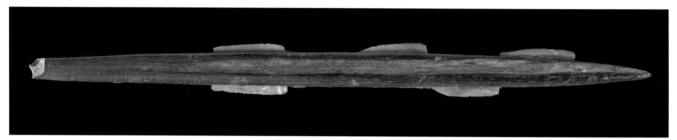

Weapon head made of microliths stuck into a bone shaft. Found in a Danish peat bog.
©*Trustees of the British Museum*

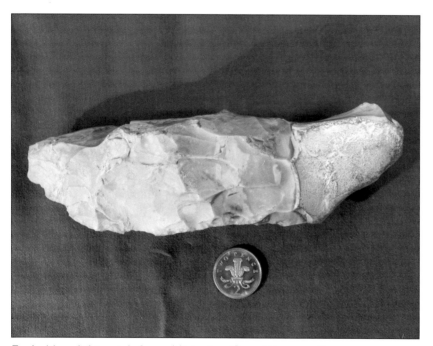

Early Mesolithic pick from Misterton Carr. Wear on the cortex (right) shows this tool was hafted.
DJB/DOM

Tools for woodworking such as axes and adzes also first appeared in the Mesolithic period. They were sharpened by a single blow made at right angles to the cutting edge, resulting in distinctive sharpening flakes. This technique helps to distinguish Mesolithic flaked axes (known as tranchet axes) from those of the Neolithic period. There were also a range of other heavy duty core tools such as picks which could have been used for a variety of purposes, from carpentry to digging.

As well as the stone artefacts, bone and antler was still widely used for tools. Many finely worked harpoon heads with multiple barbs were produced at Star Carr and they are likely to have been common components of the early Mesolithic tool kit. However, while many late

Later Mesolithic antler harpoon from the Trent
at Long Eaton or Thrumpton.
DJB/NCMG

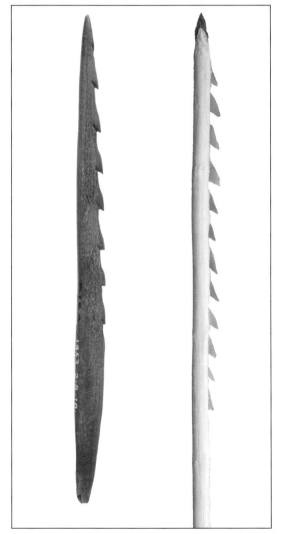

Early Mesolithic antler harpoon from Star Carr (left)
and reconstruction of a later Mesolithic version, made
of flint microliths stuck into a wooden shaft (right).
©Trustees of the British Museum/DJB

Upper Palaeolithic harpoon heads were highly decorated, most Mesolithic examples were not. Also found at Star Carr were mattocks and picks, used for digging and made of elk antler.

By the later Mesolithic period blade production was still the object, but both blades and cores had become tiny. This probably represents a change in hunting equipment. The arrangement of some microliths found preserved in peat suggests that they were attached to wooden shafts so that that they looked very much like the carved bone and antler harpoons of the early Mesolithic period, with many small barbs along the shaft. These required far less time and effort to make than their antler equivalents and would have been easily repaired too, since if the stone barbs were damaged they could be quickly replaced, which would be impossible for a barbed point made from a single piece of antler.

Tranchet axes seem to have gone out of use in the later Mesolithic period, but a new tool type, worked by drilling instead of flaking, began to be produced. These pierced pebble mace heads were not common, with less than 10 reported so far from Nottinghamshire. It is not known precisely what they were used for and suggestions range from maces for fighting or hunting through to use as weights on digging sticks. Given the sheer amount of effort required to drill a hole through a piece of stone using the technology of the time they must have been rare and costly items, making a statement about the power and status of the owner. There is also some evidence that they were used for fighting, as human skulls with fractures that could have been caused by such a weapon have been found in northern Europe.

Making a living

Mesolithic people lived mainly by hunting and gathering. Isotope studies of the few bits of human bone we have from the early Mesolithic period show that animal protein played the most important part in their diet. Marine resources and fish hardly seem to have been consumed, while plant material took a secondary role behind meat. At Star Carr, food waste showed that people were exploiting red deer, roe deer, elk, wild boar and aurochs, along with water birds such as ducks, grebes, divers and cranes.

The newly wooded environment of the Mesolithic period led to new problems in obtaining food, but also provided many new opportunities. Woodland cover disrupted the predictable movement of large herds of animals; some moved north following the retreat of the ice and those which remained were no longer found in large herds, but instead lived scattered throughout the woods. This behaviour required a change of hunting strategy and technology. The mass killing of herds at concentration points such as river crossings or valleys by groups of hunters using spears, as practised in the Upper Palaeolithic period, was no longer possible. The bow and arrow had already arrived in Northern Europe at the end of the Palaeolithic period and was a more suitable technology for hunting in woodland. Domesticated dogs had also first appeared in the Upper Palaeolithic period and were widely used in the Mesolithic period, most likely for hunting.

An early Mesolithic hunter.
His equipment is based on finds from peat bogs.
Dominic Andrews: © www.archaeoart.co.uk

Hunters now had to stalk individual animals as and when they encountered them in the forest, or to go out searching for them. They then had to get close enough to shoot arrows into the prey without hitting tree trunks or vegetation. However, arrows are less likely to kill larger animals outright, being lighter and having less penetrating power than spears. Having shot a few arrows into the intended prey the hunter would then have to track the wounded animal as it fled, eventually closing in to fire more arrows and resume the chase or being able to get close enough to deliver the killing blow. There are a number of examples where animal bones have been found with microliths embedded in them, showing how they had been attacked and in some cases, had escaped and healed. Aurochs bones from a late Mesolithic palaeochannel at Staythorpe show cut marks made by flint tools, proving that hunters were able to bring down the largest and fiercest beasts they encountered. The aurochs finally became extinct worldwide when the last individual died in Poland in the 17th century but the species had been hunted so extensively that it had become very rare in Britain by Neolithic times and was extinct here by the Bronze Age.

In addition to animal foods the forests provided a bounty of edible plant foods. Most of these leave no trace in the archaeological record. However, hazelnut shells are very durable and broken and burnt hazelnut shells have been found, often in vast quantities, on Mesolithic sites. Cooking hazelnuts allows them to be kept for much longer periods before they go off and they are highly nutritious. On sites where preservation is good other edible plant remains, such as burnt raspberry seeds, have also been found.

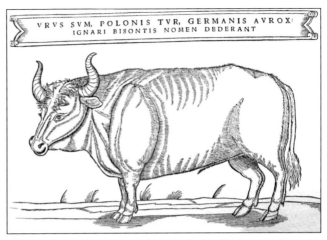

A woodcut of an aurochs made by Sigismund von Herberstein in 1556, before these animals became extinct.
Creative Commons

People faced challenges obtaining food in the changed conditions and found ways to manipulate the environment to increase their chances of success in the hunt. At Star Carr, people regularly burnt the reeds which surrounded the lake. This made it easier to get a good view of animals and birds coming to the lake to drink and also increased the chances of getting a quick kill, since it was further for prey attacked near the shore to run to reach cover. In these cleared areas it would be possible to use spears, with their superior killing power.

By the later Mesolithic period, charcoal indicating widespread forest fires appears in the archaeological record. It seems that people were clearing and burning parts of the forest in order to improve the food resources available to them. As well as the benefits to hunting, clearings in a forest promote fresh growth which attracts animals from the surrounding area. Additionally, if the fire is fierce enough to remove the tree cover, understorey shrubs flourish in the following years, providing large crops of hazelnuts and other plant foods. High concentrations of ivy pollen have been found on some later Mesolithic sites. Ivy provides good food for animals over winter and it is possible that groups were collecting ivy in order to attract animals into a particular area. With these sorts of activities already underway it would not have been a great leap for Mesolithic people to go one step further and adopt the practices of more developed farming when they came into contact with the first pioneer farmers, at the start of the Neolithic period.

People seem to have moved throughout very large territories at this time. Early Mesolithic culture covered a large area of northern Europe with the rich plains of Doggerland at its heart. The coasts, estuaries, rivers and lakes of Doggerland supplied a bounty of animal and plant foods to exploit, with other resources available in the uplands and more marginal areas. It seems that groups would move in a seasonal pattern to exploit the different resources of the landscape as they became available. Apart from animal and plant resources, other items were also collected. Good quality flint was sought after and was often transported over large distances, as were "luxury goods" such as amber, used for jewellery.

In the more marginal lands of what is now Britain winter base camps were sited in the wooded lowlands, often near rivers or lakes, or on the coast, to allow access to the wide range of resources which could be found there. The tools left behind at these sites suggest that, as well as hunting, people spent much of their time gathering raw materials and making and repairing tools and equipment. In summer they moved into the more open highlands to hunt animals which bred there, particularly red deer which were an important part of the Mesolithic economy. Tools left at these sites tend to include a high proportion of microliths, mostly used for making projectiles and so suggesting that hunting was a major activity at these camps. The Mesolithic sites we know of in Nottinghamshire have low proportions of microliths and so probably were winter lowland camps where manufacturing was taking place, rather than summer hunting camps, which may well have been in what is now Derbyshire.

At Misterton Carr, a scatter of thousands of flints was located on top of a long sand ridge next to a meander of the River Idle. This site appears to have been a base camp, the main lowland occupation site of a group using the area as part of their seasonal rounds. Smaller parties set out from the main camp to procure various resources, raw materials and to hunt, but would all gather back at base camp on completion of their particular task. A site excavated at Misson, five kilometres away, seems to have been one such satellite camp. Amongst the activities carried out at Misterton, the occupants were obtaining raw materials for the

Excavation of a tree throw at Misson, which contained 3,500 flints from the early Mesolithic.
© *Northern Archaeological Associates*

year ahead. Somewhere nearby was a source of Wolds flint, which was collected and worked here, and it has been suggested that the tools knapped here were then taken to sites in the summer hunting grounds in the uplands of Derbyshire.

By the later Mesolithic patterns of movement were changing. Isolation from the continent due to the rising seas led to changes in technology and the development of the local, British Mesolithic culture. Increased population densities, due to a growing population and to the influx of people displaced as Doggerland was drowned, seem to have resulted in much smaller territories for groups to move through. Later Mesolithic occupation sites are generally smaller in size than earlier ones, suggesting changes in the way people lived.

These pressures led to ever more human modification of the landscape. An increasing range of food sources were used in the later Mesolithic, including much more use of marine resources. On the coasts of Britain, large shell middens began to grow as people returned to the same spot time after time for hundreds of years and discarded their food waste of bones and shells in the same location.

Over exploitation led to the loss of some species, notably the elk, which was hunted to extinction around this time.

In Nottinghamshire, two sites of this date have been found. At Tiln a dense cluster of flintwork some 100 metres by 170 metres was found on a promontory running beside the River Idle. This location, and the range of tools found, suggest that this was one of the lowland home bases of later Mesolithic hunters. At Staythorpe, later Mesolithic remains were found in a river channel which was silting up between 6,800 and 6,000 years ago. The environmental evidence showed that there was oak and birch woodland beside the floodplain, with a range of smaller shrubs such as hazel, sloe, elder and dogwood and some damp grassland. Willow and alder carr grew on the floodplain. Insects and fungi associated with decaying wood suggested that fallen trees were common and charcoal was also found. As well as this valuable evidence about the late Mesolithic landscape, discoveries were also made about the activities of the people who lived here. A number of animal bones were found, including red deer and aurochs, showing signs of butchery. A red deer antler with cut marks was also recovered. This was probably being cut up to make into some kind of tool but was discarded or lost for some reason before completion.

Most significant of all was the discovery of a human leg bone from a late Mesolithic woman. Human remains from the Mesolithic are exceptionally rare, and this bone is the only piece from the whole of Nottinghamshire. Chemical analysis of the bone has shown that the Staythorpe Woman lived mostly by hunting. The protein in her diet came almost exclusively from meat during the last ten years of her life, while plant foods played very little part in her diet and she does not seem to have eaten fish at all. Whether this is because her group were purely hunters and not gatherers, or if it was her personal preference, is something we cannot know.

Travel and transport

Movement within woodland with thick understorey vegetation is very difficult and in wildwood it may not have been possible to penetrate far inland. Rivers and watercourses were probably the main routes of travel; an object that appears to be a paddle from Star Carr suggests coracles or canoes may have been used (though none have yet been found). The first arrival of people in Ireland in this period also suggests that people were using boats. Native Americans used to burn understorey vegetation to allow freer movement through wooded areas and this may have been another reason for this practice by Mesolithic people.

Housing

People in the late Upper Palaeolithic period made use of caves and rock shelters but also probably used small temporary shelters and tents. In contrast, Mesolithic people preferred to live away from caves (although the shelter of Creswell Crags was briefly used by one group of Mesolithic hunters as they passed through) and they constructed the first houses and built the first monumental architecture in Britain.

Such structures are extremely rare, and most excavated British early Mesolithic sites are represented purely by a scatter of worked flint. However, at Star Carr waterlogged conditions preserved a platform or causeway extending from the former shore into the waters of a lake. The platform was constructed from skilfully split planks and is the oldest example of carpentry in the whole of Northern Europe. There were also traces of a small round house, built using posts. It had a sunken floor carpeted with moss and contained a hearth. The discovery of many tranchet axes in Britain also suggests that woodworking skills were widespread. However it seems that mostly people lived in tents or wigwams (like recent Native American groups) which could easily be transported as they moved about. The pits, post and stake holes which are sometimes discovered on Mesolithic sites may represent the remains of such temporary structures.

At Misson in north Nottinghamshire, on a site by the River Idle, an early Mesolithic knapping scatter lay in the base

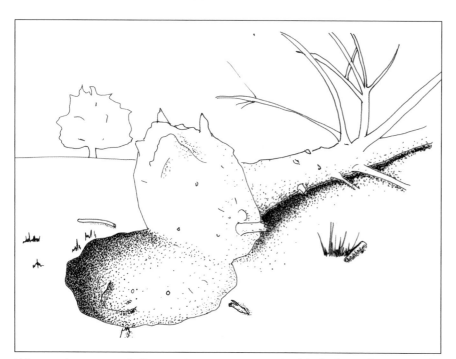

When a large tree falls over it can create a sizable hole in the ground, which can be used to make a shelter.
DJB

of a tree throw. These features are created when a large tree has fallen over, lifting its roots up and leaving a hollow in the earth. They seem to have been used fairly regularly by early people, as they can provide a very effective shelter with the addition of a couple of stakes and some animal skins.

By the later Mesolithic period, there are more examples of permanent and substantial houses though they are still very rare and the majority of settlement was probably still in tents. At Howick in Northumberland post holes of a circular hut with a sunken floor, constructed around 8,000 years ago, were found on top of an eroding cliff. This structure was around six metres in diameter and was probably similar to a wigwam in appearance, though the substantial timbers used suggest it was probably roofed with turves or thatch rather than animal skins.

Reconstruction of a later Mesolithic house at Howick.
Andrew Curtis/Creative Commons

The depth of debris which had built up inside the structure and evidence of at least three major episodes of repair and rebuilding clearly show that the hut was used over a long period of time, spanning several generations. Its location near the coast overlooking a small estuary meant that its occupants could easily make use of the resources of the estuary, coastline, open sea and inland areas, which might have allowed them to live here permanently. The other known Mesolithic houses are all in similar locations, close to the richest resources. Permanent structures might also have served to claim ownership of such areas at a time when rising sea levels were covering Doggerland and forcing people to move in search of new territories.

Religion and ritual

Much of the evidence for ritual activity comes from Star Carr. The site was one of many concentrated around a former lake, Lake Flixton, formed of glacial melt water. The Star Carr site seems to have been a special place. As well as the debris from day to day life there is plenty of evidence for 'ritual' activity too, relating to red deer and water. The red deer was very important to the early Mesolithic people as a source of food, clothes and tools. A number of sections of red deer skull with the antlers still attached were found here. These had holes pierced in them and had been designed to be used as head dresses. They were originally thought to have been disguises worn by the hunters while stalking deer, but it seems more likely they were used in some kind of shamanistic ritual, probably to appease the spirits of the deer and seek success in the hunt.

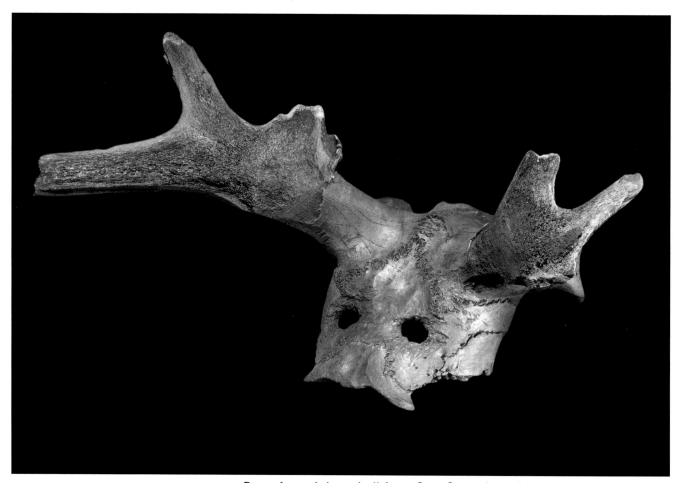

Part of a red deer skull from Star Carr, altered for use as a head-dress.
©*Trustees of the British Museum*

After use the head dresses appeared to have been deliberately deposited in the lake, and it has been suggested that the platform was built to provide access for placing objects in the water, as part of a ritual activity. During the later Bronze Age valuable objects of bronze were often placed in water and the finds at Star Carr may be evidence that this practice is considerably older. Further evidence comes from the Thames, where huge numbers of late Mesolithic axes have been found during dredging. These quantities seem far too high to be from casual loss or even rubbish disposal and they may also relate to some kind of ritual deposit in the water.

Death and burial

Animal bones are often found on Mesolithic sites but human remains are very rare. It seems that the dead were disposed of in a way that means we have not found them, either because their remains have not been preserved, or they are not in the sort of places where archaeologists usually look.

Only a few complete burials are known from Britain. One was of an adult male who was buried in the caves in Cheddar Gorge. An injury to his skull suggested he might have died violently.

There is just one early Mesolithic cemetery known in Britain, at Aveline's Hole, Somerset. A large number of individuals were laid to rest here over a short period of time, perhaps 100 years, before the cave was sealed at the end of its use. It was not reopened again until it was discovered in the 18th century, when "up to 100 bodies, laid promiscuously on the floor" were reported. They had grave goods of pierced animal teeth jewellery and fossil ammonites, and red ochre had been spread on some of the bodies.

A few other human remains have been found, mostly in caves. These tend to be just single bones, and it seems that bodies were allowed to decompose before the disarticulated bones were disposed of. Odd bones are sometimes found deposited in later Mesolithic shell middens on the coast, but there are so few that they can only represent a tiny proportion of the population. Rather than being the results of cannibalism, these deposits seem to have something to do with the special character of the middens, where waste material was deliberately placed in a small area over long periods of time, sometimes hundreds of years.

One Nottinghamshire site provides a valuable hint as to how the majority of the Mesolithic dead may have been disposed of. The discovery of a human leg bone in an old river channel at Staythorpe may suggest that rivers were the place of burial for the dead. If this were the case it would explain why so few of the population have ever been found. The action of being rolled around in the river would break most bones into tiny, unrecognisable pieces which would be swept downstream to the sea.

Use of water to dispose of the dead could be related to rising sea levels. As Doggerland, the heartland of early Mesolithic culture and the lands where their ancestors lived, hunted and died was lost under the rising water, this may have lead to the belief that water was the home of the ancestors. Putting bodies or parts of bodies into rivers may have been seen as a way of sending the dead to join them.

Catastrophe and Conflict

The loss of the rich habitats of Doggerland must have had a massive effect on people at the time, both in terms of the physical loss of land and how they thought about their world. The many legends about lands lost to the sea and great floods found throughout the world, including the legends of Atlantis and the Biblical Great Flood, may have their roots in ancient stories passed down from this time when the rising waters drowned low-lying lands around the globe.

To the Mesolithic people the effects of the rise would have sometimes been terrifyingly fast. When waters breached a natural obstacle, such as a range of hills, the lower lying land behind would be swamped very quickly, and any settlements or camps and their occupants might be swept away by the floods. More generally, people would have seen the forests in which they and their ancestors had hunted dying off as the salt waters advanced. At Goldcliff, when people were making the tracks through the mud (see above), the upright stumps of the dead trees around them would have shown how their world was changing.

There were also occasional major disasters. Around 8,000 years ago, as a result of the changes taking place as the climate warmed, a large part of the continental shelf of Norway collapsed. This led to a series of massive tsunamis radiating out from the epicentre and rushing towards the coast of Doggerland and Britain. Sediments of sand and stones deposited by the massive waves are found across Scotland up to 50 miles inland from the current coast. All settlement near the coast would have been wiped out and coastal resources devastated.

The drowning of the plains of Doggerland forced people to migrate to the margins, such as Britain. On the continent there is evidence that these increased population densities led to violence and warfare. People buried in a number of Mesolithic cemeteries in Germany, Denmark and Sweden show numerous injuries, many fatal, which were sustained during hand to hand conflict or were caused by arrows. This conflict was most likely over resources. Imagine a group moving through their territory on their seasonal rounds. They arrive in their ancestral summer hunting grounds, only to find a new group has moved in and is using up the resources. Violence is likely to have been the result.

Art

Very little in the way of art is known from the Mesolithic. Certainly, Mesolithic people did not continue the fine artistic traditions of sculpting and cave painting of the Upper Palaeolithic period. They do not seem to have decorated their tools either, for while Upper Palaeolithic bone and antler points were sometimes highly decorated, early Mesolithic examples were not.

The very small quantity of known Mesolithic art is of a very different character to that of the Palaeolithic period. Instead of the realistically drawn animals, Mesolithic 'art' does not appear to be attempting to depict objects at all and is instead very abstract. In Aveline's Hole, a cave used for burial in the early Mesolithic period, there is some engraving which may be of this date. This consists of a series of intersecting lines forming a number of 'X' shapes. Similar designs are known from early Mesolithic sites in northern France, Germany and Denmark.

Engraved lines on the walls of Aveline's Hole.
Andrew Atkinson/UBSS

The disappearance of the fine figurative art of the Upper Palaeolithic may tell us something about its purpose. If it was indeed intended as a way of leaving messages for future visitors about the resources to be found in an area, then the disappearance of the large migrating herds and the smaller ranges of the human population would have made such messages redundant.

The scarcity of art might suggest that the Mesolithic period was a dull, drab time. However this was probably not the case. The discovery of beads of various types of stone and amber, along with pierced animal teeth show that people were adorning themselves. It seems likely that they also used their artistic talents on materials which don't survive in the archaeological record, such as wood and fur. The discovery at Star Carr of a piece of red ochre which had been scored suggests that paint was being used. The score marks resulted from someone scraping the ochre with a flint tool to create a fine red powder, which when mixed with water

creates a good red paint. This could then have been used to paint wooden objects, for drawing designs on clothing or even as body paint. There are examples of painted pebbles from sites on the Continent, though what they were used for remains a mystery.
(See colour plate, page 37)

The massive changes which took place through the course of the Mesolithic period gradually led to the emergence of Britain as a number of islands, with a climate very similar to what we have today, and with a population who lived here permanently. The next major change came about as that population took on new ways of life, and started the process of changing the face of the land by growing crops and keeping domesticated animals. From this time onwards, developments in human behaviour and technology are the milestones in the story of Britain.

Neolithic

The Neolithic period saw possibly the greatest social transformation in the whole of prehistory. There was a fundamental change from the hunting and gathering way of life of the Mesolithic period, towards farming crops and keeping domestic livestock. Associated with this change were many new types of artefacts, including sickles, querns, polished stone axes and most importantly, pottery. New types of monuments first appeared during the Neolithic period, including some truly permanent settlements and ceremonial monuments such as henges and tombs as well as industrial sites such as flint mines and stone axe factories.

The Neolithic period in Britain lasted for approximately 2,000 years, starting around 4,500 BC and ending around 2,000 BC. It is sub-divided into the early Neolithic from around 4,500 to 3,000 BC, and the late Neolithic around 3,000 to 2,000 BC.

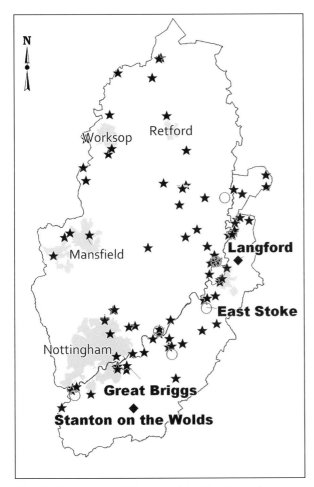

Neolithic sites and finds in Nottinghamshire
◆ = settlements
○ = henges and timber circle
★ = all other sites and finds
Contains Ordnance Survey data
© Crown copyright and database right 2011

Agriculture originated in the Near East around 10,000 years ago (8,000 BC). From there it spread to Europe via the Mediterranean, reaching south-eastern Europe about 6,000 BC and northern Europe by about 5,000 BC. Sometime after 5,000 BC the first evidence for farming began to appear in Britain and it spread to the whole of the British Isles over the next 2,000 years. The way that farming came to Britain is not certain; it was previously believed that it was due to the migration of groups of farmers from the continent, but that may be too simplistic. As there was almost certainly communication across the channel at this time, the coastal communities of Britain must have been aware of the development of farming on the continent, and may simply have copied those practices. The most likely answer lies somewhere in between these two views, with farming spreading throughout Britain by various means involving both immigration and local adoption and change.

At this time, people in Britain lived in small family groups, in dispersed farmsteads. Later on, as the population grew, regional groups began to emerge, forming the first tribes and resulting in the construction of the first large communal monuments. The planning and construction of these massive monuments would need some kind of organisation and control and this suggests that there might have been elite groups in society by this time.

Climate and Environment

At the beginning of the Neolithic period much of the British landscape was wooded. Features that we associate with the rural environment today, such as fields, trackways and villages, simply did not exist. Pollen analysis shows the woodland was dominated by alder, oak, elm and hazel. The climate was slightly warmer than today, with longer growing seasons and favourable conditions for the early farmers. They grew a combination of cereals such as wheat and barley, and kept animals such as cattle, sheep and pigs. Hunting and gathering still played a significant part in their way of life.

These early farming communities cleared significant areas in the woodland and forest during this period. Almost every pollen sequence so far studied in Britain shows falling levels of tree pollen in the centuries around 3,000 BC. A steep decrease in pollen from elm trees is so widespread that it is known as the 'elm decline'. By around 2,500 BC large areas of land and many river valleys such as the Trent valley contained substantial clearings. However, woodland clearance was nothing new, as it had been carried out by Mesolithic hunter-gatherers.

Tools and Technology

Finely flaked 'laurel leaf' from Averham
Nottinghamshire County Council

The arrival of farming fundamentally changed the relationship between people and the environment, and the tools in use also changed significantly. Stone tools were still essential, but we also have considerable amounts of other materials from this period, showing that people were using pottery, bone, antler, wood and skin.

Stone tools
Stone of various sorts remained a vital material for making tools. There were changes in technology, as the new way of life required some new types of tools, the most important being the axe.

A basic Neolithic stone tool kit included implements for tasks such as cutting (knives, serrated flakes and sickles), scraping and hide preparation (scrapers), piercing (points and burins), burnishing (fabricators) and a new form of leaf-shaped arrowhead, made using fine pressure-flaking. Far more heavy-duty tools now also came into use, such as axes, adzes and chisels, used for felling trees and woodworking. There were also quern stones for grinding grain and flint sickles for harvesting. Some of these sickles have a characteristic "silica gloss" along the cutting edge, resulting from cutting through cereal stems.

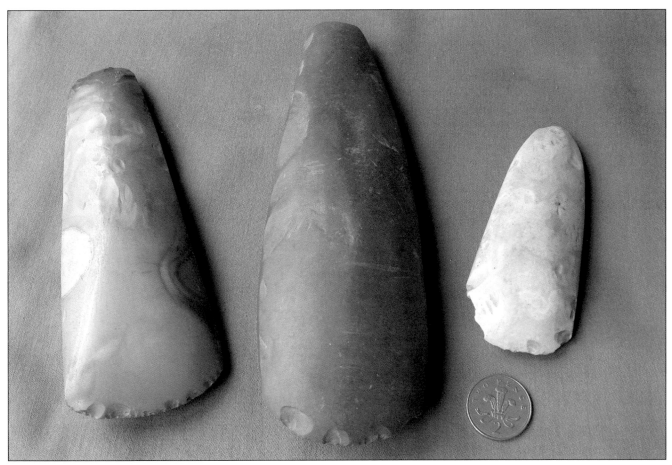

Neolithic polished axes from Holme Pierrepont (left and centre) and Bulwell (right).
DJB/NCMG

One distinctive aspect of Neolithic stonework technology, found very rarely in the Mesolithic period, was the finishing of some items by grinding and polishing, to produce smooth regular surfaces. This produced a more durable cutting edge, and it also created objects of great visual appeal, and was often used on items that appear to have been exchanged or used as symbols of status, such as axes.

Pottery

People first began to make pottery vessels in the Neolithic period, marking a great leap forward in the manufacture of objects, the control of fire and the expression of creativity. Early pottery from Britain shows a high level of sophistication and skill, so it seems that the techniques for producing it were introduced from the continent rather than having developed here. Most pottery was made locally, but there is some evidence that certain pottery types were traded over long distances.

Pottery is very durable and survives for many centuries in all sorts of conditions, and this makes it extremely important to archaeologists. Also it has frequently changed in shape and decoration over time, making it very useful for dating sites, and the different types of Neolithic pottery help to provide the framework for developments in this period.

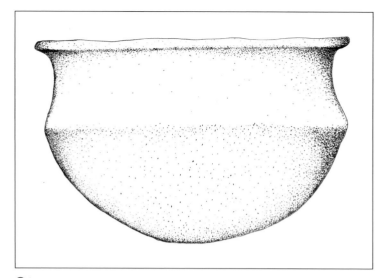

Early Neolithic pottery in Britain was similar to types found on the continent. These early pots tend to have open shapes and round bases with little or no decoration, and are known as Grimston ware after a site in Yorkshire.

From the middle of the third millennium BC there was an increase in the amount of decorated pottery, with the emergence of two main types; Peterborough ware and Grooved ware.

Grimston ware
DJB

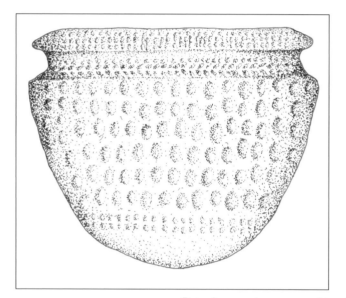

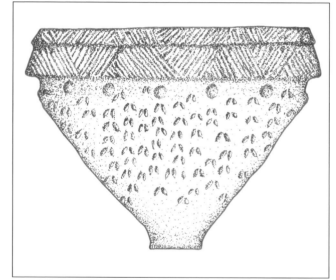

Peterborough wares – Mortlake and Fengate styles *EG*

Peterborough ware has heavy rims and elaborate impressed decoration. Three different types have been identified; Ebbsfleet (none so far found in Nottinghamshire), Mortlake, and Fengate. The Ebbsfleet style has simple decoration, consisting mainly of incisions with some simple impressions. Cross-hatching and herringbone are the most popular motifs. In the Mortlake style the decoration becomes more elaborate and varied. Twisted and whipped cord impressions are common, as are bone, stick, and fingernail impressions. The pots often have a high waist which constricts the neck. In the Fengate style rims become deeper, forming a heavy collar. The bases are flat, and so small in relation to the high and wide shape of the pots that they would be unsteady and they may have been suspended instead. Radiocarbon dating indicates that all three types were in use much at the same time.

Grooved ware has grooved, incised and applied decoration and the pots are tub and bucket-shaped with wide, flat bases. It seems to have appeared sometime after 3,200 BC, and there were various regional types, however none has so far been found in Nottinghamshire. Interestingly, grooved ware is often found on henge sites.

Antler, Bone and Wood

Materials such as wood, bark, plant fibres and leather were widely used for everyday objects in the Neolithic period, as shown by the artefacts discovered with Ötzi the Iceman. While only a small amount of Neolithic woodwork has survived in Britain, there is enough to give us some idea of how much wood was used. Wooden finds include dugout canoes and paddles, as well as extensive trackways in marshy areas, the most famous being the Sweet Track on the Somerset levels. Many flint and stone tools and weapons of course had wooden handles or shafts. Evidence for the extensive use of wood in buildings comes in the form of post-holes on both settlement and burial sites as well as ceremonial monuments such as timber circles.

Bone and antler were also used for tool production, and are found more often because of their durability. A tremendous number of antler picks and ox scapula shovels used for digging and quarrying have been recovered from Neolithic flint mines and henge ditches. Antler combs were probably used to strip hair from hides and bone points were probably used as awls to pierce them for sewing. Bone skewer pins are often found with burials along with simple antler pins and beads. Unfortunately, the use of other organic materials such as furs for clothing, reeds for baskets and matting, and leather for containers, cloths and other uses can only be guessed at.

Bone pin, believed to be Neolithic, from Creswell Crags.
DJB/CHT

The Missing Evidence

Our understanding of the Neolithic depends very much on the evidence that survives. This usually consists of pottery, worked bone and flint tools. Sadly, unless it is preserved in unusual circumstances such as waterlogged sites, precious organic material simply rots away and is lost. A glimpse of these missing artefacts was provided in 1991 when Ötzi the Iceman, a frozen mummy dating from the late Neolithic period, was discovered high in the mountains near the border between Austria and Italy.

This discovery was of particular importance as he came to us straight from his everyday life. For the first time we have the complete equipment of a prehistoric person. It should come as no surprise that the Iceman was fully equipped for his trip into the high mountains. He also carried what he needed to repair or replace any piece of equipment which got damaged or lost. He had a total of 18 different types of wood, using the most appropriate type of wood for each tool. If the body had been buried in normal conditions then all that would have survived would have been a few flint blades and arrowheads along with his copper axe. However, because of the frozen conditions it was possible to recover his cloak, hat, loincloth, leggings, shoes, shirt, a longbow and a quiver full of arrows, a hafted copper axe, a flint knife with wooden sheath, a wooden-framed backpack, two bark containers, a belt pouch and a medicine bag. This unique and spectacular discovery clearly illustrates how little we normally have to go on in terms of surviving artefacts. (See colour plate inside back cover)

Making a Living

By about 3,000 BC the hunter-gatherer groups had all but vanished, except for in a few coastal and northern regions. So what became of them? It used to be thought that the change from the Mesolithic period to the Neolithic period in the British Isles was a rapid process. However, the previous way of life based on hunting and gathering had been going on in western Europe for around half a million years, and it seems unlikely that it would be swept away so quickly. Early farming was probably much harder work than hunting and gathering, but it is likely that one of the main reasons for making the change was the increasing population. Mesolithic hunters had already been 'managing' the wild herds on which they depended, by making clearings in woodland around sources of drinking water and perhaps by providing fodder. So for many people, the transition from managed hunting to keeping domesticated animals may not have been such a dramatic change, and it provided them with a more reliable source of food. It would appear that the resident Mesolithic hunter-gatherers willingly chose to adopt the new way of life.

Animal husbandry was practised throughout Britain and bones of domesticated animals including cattle, pigs, sheep and goats are found on the earliest Neolithic sites. The first domesticated animals were much smaller than the native strains of Britain and they must have been imported from continental Europe. On sites in southern England the bones of cattle are the most common, followed by sheep. In the Midlands region cattle still came first but pigs were far more important than sheep. Since cattle and pigs prefer to browse in woodland it is possible that the midlands had more tree cover than elsewhere. Studies of the age and sex of the cattle from several Neolithic sites have found a high percentage of adult females, so they may well have been farmed for milk as well as meat. By the late Neolithic period there seems to have been a change of emphasis from mixed agriculture towards more herding; there is less evidence for cereals, while the number of animals, particularly pigs, increased.

These small, hardy sheep from the island of Soay in Scotland are believed to be very similar to Neolithic sheep.
©iStockphoto.com/whitemay

Traces of Neolithic crops have been found that have been charred or preserved in waterlogged sites and impressions of seeds are sometimes found on pottery vessels. Emmer and einkorn wheat were the staple crops but naked and hulled barley was also grown. These early varieties of grain were much closer genetically to wild grasses. Flint sickles were used to harvest the crops, and saddle-shaped stone querns to grind the grain.

Wild food was still used, whenever available. Bones of red deer, horse, wild boar, wild cat, badger, beaver, hare, and many other smaller animals have been recorded from Neolithic sites across Britain. Evidence for wild plant foods includes hazelnuts and crab apples, along with raspberries, blackberries and other tree and shrub fruits, and roots and tubers may also have been collected.

In the past few years, a number of "burnt mounds" of late Neolithic and Bronze Age date have been found in Nottinghamshire. They are situated close to former channels and tributaries of the River Trent, and include examples at Girton and Gonalston. These structures were possibly used for cooking. They consist of a mound of shattered stones and charcoal, often with an adjacent hearth and trough. The trough could be rock-cut, wood-lined or clay-lined to ensure it was watertight. The shattered rock fragments are the remains of stones heated in fires, which were used to heat water for cooking, bathing, dyeing or even leather treatment. It is possible that many were used for several different functions.

Trade and Transport

Early farming communities did not exist in isolation. Rivers provided routes for travel and elsewhere a network of trackways linked one group with the next. It is clear that people could travel about and that some items, including stone axes, were traded over long distances.

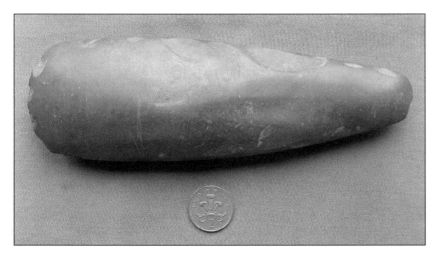

This polished axe, found at Holme Pierrepont, is made of greenstone from Langdale in the Lake District.
DJB/NCMG

The desirability of certain stones for making axes has left us with the very first traces of industrial production in Britain. In areas where flint is found, there were a number of flint mines. The flint was extracted in one of two ways: where it was close to the surface, it could be reached by simply digging shallow pits. In places where good seams of flint were located some way below the surface, mineshafts were sunk, up to 14 metres deep. Although a wide range of tools were made from the mined flint, axes were the main product.

Many Neolithic axeheads made of distinctive types of stone are found at sites far away from where that stone naturally occurs. Several so-called 'axe factories' are now known, one of the most famous being at Great Langdale in Cumbria. The stone was obtained from scree slopes and large numbers of unfinished or broken rough-outs from the early stages of the manufacture of stone axes have been found there. The rough-outs were carried away from the production site and finished by grinding and polishing elsewhere. Langdale axes are widespread and together make up nearly 20% of all stone axes found in Britain. Significantly, they are found in large numbers in regions of southern and eastern England where good quality flint suitable for axe production was readily available, and where many flint axes have also been found. So as there was no shortage of local products, it seems that the axes from Great Langdale were desirable objects and that people would go to more effort to have one.

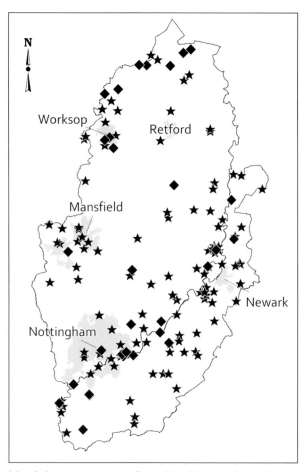

Neolithic stone axes found in Nottinghamshire
◆ = axes from Great Langdale (Group 6)
★ = axes from all other sources
Contains Ordnance Survey data © Crown copyright and database right 2011

Microscopic examination of the wear on many axes shows that they were used for felling trees and working wood. However, some axes show no sign of wear on their blades whatsoever. About 70 green jadeite axes have been found in Britain, some of which are so thin and finely polished that they would have shattered if they were ever used. They are a very good indication of the extensive network of contacts that existed at this time, as they actually originated in the Alps.

Since axes were being produced and traded in large numbers, it is highly likely that lots of other goods were also changing hands. But Neolithic trade and exchange was very different to

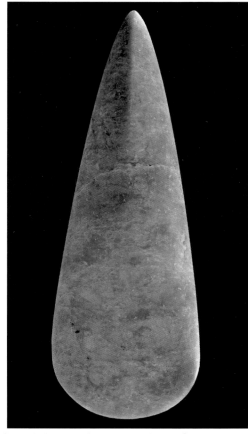

Finely polished jadeite axe, from Canterbury.
©Trustees of the British Museum

our modern notions of trade involving markets, money, buying and selling. One suggestion is that these items were exchanged from one person to another, so that many short distance exchanges resulted in an overall movement of hundreds of kilometres. Alternatively, many products may have been transported in bulk, perhaps by boat along the coast.

Housing

Archaeological evidence for settlements and houses is very sparse, with less than a dozen Neolithic houses having been found in England. Typically they consisted of small, single farmsteads sited in sheltered spots, often on well drained soils, on low hills or in river valleys. The houses themselves were similar to those in Europe, being small and rectangular, and roughly 10 metres long by 5 metres wide. The remains consist of hearths associated with a few pits, post-holes from the house or some other building, and a scatter of household debris. The walls of the houses were probably made of split logs and the pitched roof would have been of reeds or grass. Partition walls either side of a central passage divided the house into two. Smoke from the hearth seeped out through the roof which would have been high enough to avoid catching fire from sparks flying up. These settlements were presumably surrounded by fields and grazing areas.

So far, there are just a couple of examples of Neolithic settlements from Nottinghamshire. At Stanton on the Wolds, a scatter of about 200 worked flints and quantities of animal bones together with a hearth made of stones were found in a round depression. This was perhaps the site of a tree-throw, which was used to create a substantial shelter where people were processing food. Another site, at Langford, was located during work before the widening of the A46. Here there were a number of features, including pits and post holes which could be traces of structures. The finds in these features showed occupation spread over a long period of time, starting with possible Grimston ware sherds from the early Neolithic period, continuing through later Neolithic Peterborough ware and stretching into the early Bronze Age.

One of the main reasons for evidence of houses being so slight is that most Neolithic farmers still led a mobile lifestyle which did not usually include living in permanent settlements. It seems that every few years the land they farmed would reach a point where it could no longer support crops, due to the loss of soil fertility and the build up of weeds, and the people would have to move on. Each group seems to have moved around a fairly small region in this way. Similarly, it seems that they were regularly herding their livestock between different grazing areas. So it is not surprising that the houses these people lived in were slight constructions, made to be easily dismantled and moved.

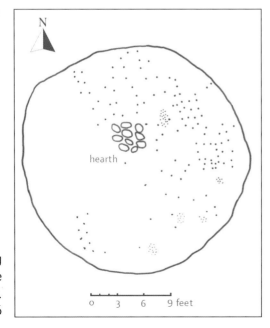

Plan of the hut at Stanton on the Wolds, showing where flint tools (large dots) and scatters of bone were found. The entrance was to the north-west.
Based on TTS 1972, vol 76, p 6

Interior of one of the Neolithic houses at Skara Brae, Orkney.
Ursilla Spence

However, there are some examples of undoubtedly permanent Neolithic settlements, in the Western and Northern Isles of Scotland. The scarcity of timber on the islands led to the use of the local sandstone for building houses and tombs which have then not been disturbed by later farming practices. This has allowed the remarkable preservation of several settlements, including the famous site of Skara Brae.

These stone houses are exceptional, and it seems that for the most part Neolithic farmers, like their Mesolithic predecessors, lived on the move, coming together only for ceremonial events. It would take many generations before farming settlements became a dominating feature of the British landscape. Until that time the only permanent structures in the landscape were the tombs and monuments.

Religion and Ritual

In contrast to the slight evidence for Neolithic domestic buildings and settlements, some Neolithic burial and ritual sites such as long barrows and henges are still imposing features in the landscape. The fact that people were prepared to spend so much effort on building these monuments says a lot about how Neolithic communities were organised and about their attitudes to death. The remains of burials found in tombs and barrows show us that Neolithic practices were very different from our own. Typically, burials of the early Neolithic period were 'collective', where the remains of many individuals were placed in a tomb or grave together, in contrast to our tradition of single burials in separate graves.

Causewayed Camps

Some of the earliest Neolithic ceremonial monuments were causewayed camps. These were large circular or oval enclosures, consisting of one or more concentric rings of banks and ditches. The ditches were dug in short sections, leaving frequent causeways in between. It isn't certain what these sites were used for, but it seems that people would gather here for ceremonies and rituals which often involved the burial of significant items, such as finely polished stone axeheads, complete pottery vessels, or human remains. One function of these sites appears to have been excarnation, a funerary practice where corpses were exposed, so that the flesh decayed in the open air before the bones were finally buried. So far, no causewayed camps have been found in Nottinghamshire.

Long Barrows and Chambered Tombs

At the same time that the camps were in use, two types of monuments were being used for burials. The main difference between the two types is the construction method: long barrows often contained timber structures, while chambered tombs contained stone-built chambers. Both types were covered by an earth mound, which generally covered a far larger area than the burial structure or chamber. The chamber could be re-entered for adding more burials, and some of these tombs were in use for a long time, being altered several times over the centuries. Each barrow contained the disarticulated remains of many people, often with many of the smaller bones missing; supporting the suggestion that excarnation was practised. It seems that Neolithic burials were complex affairs with deposit in the barrows being the final stage in a long series of rituals.

There are no signs of any chambered tombs in Nottinghamshire, and there are no long barrows surviving as earthworks. However there are just a few sites where marks in the soil may be showing us where a long barrow once stood; the earthwork has been completely ploughed away, leaving just the buried ditches that once surrounded it. A few other sites may be the remains of "mortuary enclosures", small rectangular enclosures which were apparently used for excarnation.

It is clear that the burial sites that have been investigated can't possibly have contained the remains of all the people who lived in the local area over a long period of time. Maybe the bones found in them were just those of certain favoured people, or only a few bones were thought to be necessary to honour the ancestors. But there are places where human bones have been found that had a different fate. One of these was at a gravel quarry at Langford, where an old river channel had been blocked by a log jam. Caught up in the log jam were many human and animal bones, including 13 human skulls, of men, women and children. One explanation is that the river flooded through an area where bodies were being exposed, sweeping the bones away downstream until they got trapped in the log jam.

Excavation underway at the log jam at Langford.
A human skull can be seen in the centre of the bottom shelf.
D Garton/TPA

Henge Monuments

A henge is a circular or oval enclosure consisting of a ditch and a bank, which was thrown up on the outside of the ditch. This arrangement means that they were not made for defence. They appear from the late Neolithic period and are widely distributed throughout Britain. Interestingly, henges are a monument type that is unique to the British Isles.

Every henge is unique. At one end of the scale are small pit circles or 'mini-henges' with diameters of around 10-20 metres, constructed by digging a series of joined pits to form roughly circular ditches. These are quite common in the East Midlands. At the other are the 'super-henges' such as Avebury in Wiltshire which have diameters of between 320 and 480 metres. They could have one or more entrances and some had internal stone or timber settings. Henges are not usually found on their own; they often occur in groups or 'complexes' in parts of the landscape where there were earlier monuments. They sometimes also incorporate lunar and solar alignments which must have had significance for the people who built them.

There are a number of henges in Nottinghamshire, but most have been ploughed flat and it is not possible to see them on the ground. Our nearest substantial henge is at Arbor Low in Derbyshire, which is open to the public.

Timber and Stone Circles

Timber and stone circles are part of the same monument tradition as henges, though they continued to be constructed and used well into the early Bronze Age. There are lots of theories about the geometry and possible astronomical alignments of stone circles and many of them are difficult to prove. However it does seem that some sites at least were laid out with reference to the cycles of the sun and moon, and this might have had something to do with marking the passage of the year. It appears that these circular enclosures, however they were constructed, were designed to restrict or control movement inside them, maybe for carrying out ritual activities.

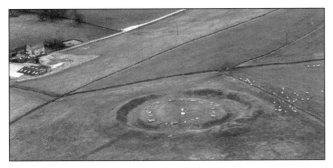

The henge and stone circle at Arbor Low, Derbyshire. *Ken Smith*

The henge at Arbor Low has a stone circle inside. So far, there is no firm evidence for any stone circles in Nottinghamshire, but there was a timber circle at East Stoke which is now only visible as a ring of dark marks on air photographs. It was a large structure, between 90 and 95 metres in diameter, with a double row of posts. There has been no excavation here, so we don't know if it was built in the Neolithic or later in the Bronze Age.

The marks in the crop left by the holes for a timber circle at East Stoke.
The maximum diameter of the circle was 95 metres.
CUCAP – ref DC10

Recent excavations in Nottinghamshire have found a number of sites that seem to fit in this tradition of circular monuments. A circular ditch 27 metres across was found south of Saxondale during works on the Fosse Way. It had once had a bank around the outside, like a very small henge, and Bronze Age burials had been placed in the ditch after it had silted up. Another circular structure at Great Briggs, Holme Pierrepont was originally thought to be the site of a Bronze Age round barrow. Excavation revealed a series of circular ditches, with the smallest ditch being the earliest, followed by six or so later ones, each larger than the one before. Early Neolithic Grimston ware was found in the ring ditches and also in a number of pits inside them. A range of other artefacts were recovered, including polished stone axes and early Neolithic flints. There were also later finds, suggesting that the site was still being visited in the late Neolithic period and early Bronze Age.

Cursus Monuments
Cursus monuments consist of pairs of long parallel banks, up to 100 metres wide with external ditches and often with squared-off ends. They vary tremendously in length, from as little as 50 metres to over 10 kilometres long. They don't usually have any internal features, but they sometimes incorporate previously existing long barrows into their alignments. Around 100 examples are known and many more probably remain to be discovered. These monuments are very poorly dated and understood. The name "cursus" was given to them by early antiquaries who thought that they were ancient race tracks for chariots. While the precise functions of cursus monuments remain unclear, their link with long barrows suggests they might be associated with the rituals of death and burial. Marks that could be the fragmentary traces of a cursus have been spotted at Newton, near Bingham.

Art

There are a number of carvings dating from the Neolithic on stones inside chambered tombs and passage graves, and also on rocks in the open. These often include spiral patterns and circles, but not humans or animals. A few carved chalk figurines have been found in the flint mines, and there are also some carved stone balls, cylinders and other shapes, of unknown use. Apart from this most creativity seems to have been spent on decorating pottery, and perhaps on the finely polished stone axes that were meant for show rather than use. Of course it is almost certain that other objects were also decorated, from clothing to the posts of the timber circles.

By around 2,000 BC the Neolithic period was at an end. Later Neolithic styles of pottery such as Grooved ware were no longer being made or used. Instead, from about 2,300 BC a new type of pottery had appeared, which originated on the continent. Along with this new Beaker pottery tradition came a range of other objects and technologies previously unknown in Britain, including barbed and tanged flint arrowheads, perforated stone battleaxes and the first metal objects, in the form of copper knives and ornaments of gold. There were also dramatic changes in ritual practices. Unlike the collective burials of the early Neolithic period, which emphasised the ancestors and community, burials increasingly consisted of a single burial with grave goods under round barrows. Although there were many other aspects of life which continued, these changes are taken to mark the beginning of the Bronze Age.

Further Reading

Prehistory

Barton, Nicholas. 1997. *Stone Age Britain*.
English Heritage, B T Batsford. ISBN 0 7134 6846 7

Megaw, JVS and Simpson, DDA, 1979. *Introduction to British Prehistory*,
Leicester University Press, Barnes and Noble. ISBN 0 389 20982 1

Mithen, Steven, 2003. *After the ice. A global human history*.
Orion Books. ISBN 978 0 7538 1392 8

Stringer, Chris, 2006. *Homo Britannicus*.
Penguin. ISBN 0 713 99795 8

Lithic Technology

Butler, Chris. 2005. *Prehistoric Flintwork*.
Tempus Publishing. ISBN 0 7524 3340 7.

Waddington, Clive, 2004. *The Joy of Flint (An introduction to stone tools and guide to the Museum of Antiquities collection)*.
Museum of Antiquities, University of Newcastle Upon Tyne. ISBN 0 7017 0165 X

Doggerland

Gaffney, V, Fitch, S and Smith, D. 2009. *Europe's Lost World. The Rediscovery of Doggerland*.
CBA Research Report 160. CBA. ISBN978 1 902771 77 9

Trent Valley in all periods

Knight, David, and Howard, Andy J, 2004. *Trent Valley Landscapes*.
Heritage Marketing and Publications Ltd. ISBN 0 9544456 4 3.

Places To Visit

Please check with the venue for current opening times.

Creswell Crags Museum and Heritage Centre
Crags Road, Welbeck, Worksop,
Nottinghamshire, S80 3LH.
01909 720378
www.creswell-crags.org.uk

Includes a visitor centre with café, shop, and museum containing displays and artefacts from all periods of Palaeolithic occupation in the caves. Also has the caves and cave art.
No charge for access to gorge, cave tours and museum have admission fee (see website).
Cave tours run at weekends and school holidays only.

Arbor Low Henge
Just off the minor road which leads from Parsley Hey to Youlgrave. Parsley Hey lies on the A515 Buxton-Ashbourne road, about 12km south of Buxton. There is parking along the side of the lane leading to the farm which lies below Arbor Low. There is an 'honesty' box at the farm in which you are requested to pay £1 per visitor.
Open all year.

Derby Museum and Art Gallery
The Strand, Derby, DE1 1BS
01332 641901.
http://www.derby.gov.uk/LeisureCulture/MuseumsGal leries/Derby_Museum_and_Art_Gallery.htm

Good prehistoric galleries including large assemblage of Lower Palaeolithic material from the Trent Valley and much Middle Palaeolithic from Creswell Crags.
Free admission.

Doncaster Museum and Art Gallery
Chequer Road, Doncaster, DN1 2AE.
01302 735409
http://www.doncaster.gov.uk/museums/

Good galleries with quite a bit of North Nottinghamshire material, particularly Mesolithic and Neolithic from Misterton Carr.
Free admission.

University of Nottingham Museum
University Park, Nottingham, NG7 2RD
01159 514815
http://www.nottingham.ac.uk/museum

Small quantity of Palaeolithic to Neolithic material on display.

Free admission but may be a charge for parking on University campus.